To

Jennifer

Jaume

# ROCCO'S
# 5
# MINUTE FLAVOR

**Rocco DiSpirito**

with Kris Kurek

Photographs by Henry Leutwyler
Design by Ruba Abu-Nimah

SCRIBNER
New York   London   Toronto   Sydney

SCRIBNER
1230 Avenue of the Americas
New York, NY 10020

SCRIBNER and design are trademarks of
Macmillan Library Reference USA, Inc., used under license
by Simon & Schuster, the publisher of this work.

For information about special discounts for bulk purchases,
please contact Simon & Schuster Special Sales:
1-800-456-6798  or  business@simonandschuster.com

Designed by Ruba Abu-Nimah
Text set in HTF Gotham & HTF Ziggurat

Manufactured in the United States of America

1   3   5   7   9   10   8   6   4   2

Library of Congress Cataloging-in-Publication Data is available.

ISBN-13:  978-0-7432-7384-8
ISBN-10:  0-7432-7384-2

*This book is dedicated to those of you who grab the Good Life and spread it around. The Good Life is something I talk about a lot. It's not a specific food, wine, or place. It's the space between people, it's an attitude, a state of mind where anything is possible when sharing a pure moment with friends, family, or loved ones. And of course it's up to you, the students of the good life, the aficionados of flavor, the gourmands of everyday good things, to make this a movement. From caviar to boxed brownie mix, French cheese to Cheetos, it's always good when shared.*

*To the ones who watch me on TV, like Haru from South Africa, and send me emails; like Janine from Shaker Heights, Ohio, who listens to my daily radio show, Food Talk, on WOR; like Cynthia from New Jersey and Joe from the boogie-down Bronx, who both send letters and gifts; like Rosemary from Allentown, Pennsylvania— all wanting help to gain access to those unforgettable moments that occur in the space between people, where the people don't eat foie gras every day but want to feel like they do anyway and who never drank a bottle of Lafitte 45 but share the joy of the glass and the table as if they did. With your help and my recipes, you will become an entertaining Good Life guru and, most important, entertain yourselves along the way.*

y sincerest thanks and appreciation, and a free dinner anytime and anywhere you want from me to you:

Special thanks to my partner, **Linda Lisco,** for putting up with me and putting out for me. Her skills, intelligence, persistence, and life force have filled the sails of this ship for a long time, and with her help it will be a long journey.

WOW! **Ruba Abu-Nimah.** WOW! RUBA—for loving me and what I do and of course for her immeasurable talent. She designs my books and brand with passion and care, and it shows.

**Henry Leutwyler,** for his extraordinary photographs that surpass my expectations every time. His work reaches deep within and gives us pause. He never knew he knew how to shoot food and now he can easily teach everyone else. For his sincere friendship and love. And, of course, for insisting I work with Ruba.

**Matthias Gaggl,** for his Teutonic, hair-product-loving, illest lighting, Eurodisco singing, best assistant ever bad self.

To the indescribable **Kris Kurek,** for her unbelievable skill and impeccable recipe testing, her thoughtful and much-appreciated collaboration, her ability to bust butt when needed, and for putting up with me.

The great people of Scribner, like **Beth Wareham,** for being a great editor, leader, and bookmaker; **Jill Vogel,** for painstakingly editing my manuscript; **Kate Bittman,** for being a publicist extraordinaire; and, of course, **Susan Moldow** and **Roz Lippel,** for buying in.

My friends at the William Morris agency, especially The Great **Mark Itkin,** for watching over me; **Suzy Unger,** for her creativity and tenacity; **Brooke Slavic,** for getting me good work; **Jen Walsh,** for her superstar sales skills and believing in my writing career; and **Evan, Scott,** and **Kristin,** for spreading the word.

All my friends at QVC for believing in me and giving my burgeoning lifestyle brand a great start, especially **Ken O'Brien, Donna Donnelly, Jonas Marusa, Eric Theiss,** The Genius . . . **Bob Rae,** and The Big Boss **Darlene**—can I offer Mama's Meatballs forever as step one?

My peeps at WOR, especially **Rick Buckley,** for taking a chance on a guy with absolutely no radio experience at all and being the perfect boss. To **Mike Figliola,** for being a friend and an inspiration and a great producer; **Mike Waller,** for working late nights on beats, bits, and giving us his original tracks. To **Lisa,** for being there at the beginning; **Joan,** for being a legend; **Heather,** for giving me a clue; **Jen,** for sharing my opinions with me; **Kerry,** for stopping at nothing to get us going in the mornings; **Maurice Tunick,** for his support; **Bob Bruno,** for teaching me to respect the mic and for his fashion sense.

**Laurelle Eichelberger,** for her friendship and assistance with the photography of 5MF.

**Anthony** and **Martina Gordon,** for sharing their beautiful family home with me.

To **David** and **Pernilla Avital,** for being supportive, generous, and lovely. Especially Pernilla.

To **Jason** and his friend Photoshop, for fooling the world.

**Food Emporium,** for letting us ravage their store for our photo shoot.

**My radio audience**—YOU HAVE CHANGED MY LIFE—and continue to breathe life into me every day at 11 a.m.

**My RoccoDiSpirito.com customers, fans, email buddies**—for support, great ideas, and best wishes.

**Colin Cowie** and **Stuart Brownstein,** for generously sharing their beautiful home with me.

**NYC,** for reminding me that life is full of surprise and wonder.

Last but not at all least, my family: My mama, **Nicolina,** for her support and love. My dad, **Rafaelle,** for his enthusiasm and constructive criticism. My brother, **Mike,** for embracing his brother. My sister, **Maria,** for loving me infinitely. My brother-in-law, **Jack,** for all his generosity since forever. My sister-in-law, **Patty,** for putting up with my brother. My nieces and nephews, **Mike, Andrew, Brooke,** and **Mikey Jr.,** for laughing at me.

# ROCCO'S 5 MINUTE FLAVOR

# CONTENTS

Introduction     **1**
**MENUS**     **21**

## APPETIZERS     **25**
Fresh Fast Guacamole     **26**
Warm Artichoke Parmigiano Dip     **29**
Grilled Asparagus and Oyster Mushrooms with Pecorino Cheese     **30**
Mushroom Quesadillas     **33**
New-Style Tuna Sashimi     **34**
Creamy Lemon Shrimp Salad with Cucumbers and Watercress     **35**
Fried Calamari and Artichokes with Hummus Dipping Sauce     **36**
Clams Oreganata     **37**
Mussels with Hummus Broth and Crusty Italian Bread     **38**
Firecracker Shrimp     **39**
Garlicky Lemon Shrimp     **41**
See-Thru Scallops with Lemon Brown Butter and Celery Leaves     **42**
Fennel-Seared Chicken Livers with Watercress and Oranges     **44**
Puffy Chicken with Green Curry Basil Sauce     **46**
Grilled Stuffed Veal with Basil and Provolone     **47**

## FONDUES     **49**
Sharp Cheddar and Beer Fondue with Warm Pretzels     **50**
Mushroom Fondue     **51**
Salmon and Sesame Swiss Fondue     **52**
Tuna Tempura Swiss Fondue with Wasabi Soy     **53**
Shrimp Swiss Fondue with Arrabbiata Dipping Sauce     **54**
Chicken Swiss Fondue with Dijon Sour Cream and Hummus     **56**
Duck Swiss Fondue     **57**
Beef Swiss Fondue with Three Sauces     **58**
Pigs in a Blanket Swiss Fondue     **59**

## SOUPS     **61**
Chilled Cucumber Soup with Smoked Salmon and Crème Fraîche     **62**
Rich Mushroom Bouillon     **63**
Mushroom Soup with Boursin Croutons     **64**
Stracciatella     **65**
Corn and Crab Chowder with Tarragon     **66**
Hot-and-Sour Shrimp Rice Noodle Soup     **69**
Turkey, Green Onion, and Rice Noodle Soup     **70**
Beef Shabu-Shabu with Watercress     **71**
Roast Beef Borscht     **72**
Vietnamese Beef and Basil Soup     **73**

## SALADS     **75**
Avocado Salad with Red Onion and Feta     **76**
Pico de Gallo Salad with Avocado     **77**
Goat Cheese, Radish, and Dried Cranberry Salad     **78**
Pear and Stilton Salad     **79**
Tomato and Mozzarella Salad     **80**
Charred Mackerel with Pears and Caesar Dressing     **81**

Shrimp Salad with Red Onion, Mango, and Cilantro 82

Chicken, Goat Cheese, and Blood Orange Salad 84

Buffalo Chicken Tenders with Celery and Blue Cheese Salad 85

Peanut Chicken and Radicchio Salad 86

Chicken and Chopped Salad 87

Warm Waldorf Chicken Salad 88

Chilled Pork Tenderloin Salad with Chopped Olive Dressing 89

Prosciutto, Parmigiano, Pimiento, and Arugula Salad 90

**SANDWICHES** 93

Hot Chicken and Brie Sandwich with Toasted Pecans 94

Hot Turkey "Coleslaw" Sandwich 96

Mushroom and Red Onion Burgers 100

Roast Beef Wrap with Garlic Relish 101

Ham on Rye with Artichokes and Dijon 102

Toasted Hot Dog Reuben 103

**PANINI** 105

Feta and Kalamata Panini 106

Smoked Salmon and Swiss Cheese Panini 107

Roast Beef and Boursin Panini 108

Prosciutto, Mozzarella, and Tomato Panini 109

Ham and Gorgonzola Panini 110

**SIDES** 113

All-Purpose Mushroom Mix 115

Cannellini with Tricolor Peppers, Tomato, and Parsley 116

Good Ol' Rice and Beans 118

Mamma's Vegetable Giambotta 119

Scalloped Potatoes with Gruyère Cheese and Mushrooms 120

Soft Polenta with Wild Mushrooms 121

**VEGETARIAN MAIN DISHES** 123

Basil and Potato Frittata with Frisée 124

Eggplant Parmigiano 125

Red Onion Frittata with Baby Spinach 126

Soft Scrambled Eggs with Asparagus on Toasted Croissants 127

Tofu and Red Pepper Flash-Fry 128

White Bean and Mushroom Chili 129

**PASTA AND NOODLE MAIN DISHES** 133

Rice Noodles with Spicy Peanut Sauce 134

Gnocchi with Toasted Garlic, Walnuts, and Bitter Greens 135

Capellini with Littleneck Clams 136

Capellini alla Puttanesca 139

Handkerchief Pasta with Lobster, Bok Choy, and Lemon Cream Sauce 141

Warm Chicken, Feta, and Melon Seed Pasta Salad 142

Pierogi with Ham, Dandelion Greens, and Sour Cream Mustard Sauce 145

Linguine alla Carbonara 147

Sausage Lasagna 148

**FISH AND SHELLFISH MAIN DISHES** 151

Sole with Charred Red Onions and Lemon Butter 152

Parmigiano Flounder with White Beans and Olive Tapenade 155

Sea Bass with Leeks, Chestnuts, and Dates 156

Cod Flash-Fry with Mint 158

Cod Provençal 159

Red, White, and Green Cod — 160

Trout with Butternut Squash and
Blood Oranges — 162

Cornmeal and Red Onion–Crusted Skate
with Lime Butter — 164

Black-and-Tan Salmon with Scallions — 165

Honey-Glazed Salmon with Cinnamon,
Carrots, and Chicory — 166

Salmon in Butternut Squash Barbecue Sauce — 167

Salmon with Shiitake Mushrooms
in Ginger-Soy Broth — 168

Seared Salmon with Sugar Snap Peas
and Herring — 169

Mahi-Mahi with Endive and
Orange Marmalade Glaze — 170

Grilled Squid with Coconut Broth, Leeks,
and Papaya — 171

Savory Seafood Stew — 174

Catfish and Rice Sofrito — 175

Clam Brodettatto with Chorizo and Peas — 176

Curried Mussel Fricassee — 177

Crab Cakes with Avocado Dip and Arugula Salad — 178

Sautéed Scallops with
Pickled Ginger Red Cabbage — 179

Shrimp and Broccoli Flash-Fry — 180

Shrimp and Scallion Frittata — 181

Shrimp Fra Diavolo with Couscous
and Broccoli Rabe — 182

Shrimp and Noodle Saté Sauté — 183

Shrimp Scampi with Grilled Bread — 186

Skewered Shrimp with Beans and Scallions — 187

**POULTRY MAIN DISHES** — 189

Chicken and Cauliflower Flash-Fry — 190

Chicken and Wild Mushroom Strudel — 192

Chicken with Tomato, Basil, and
Crispy Parmigiano Crackers — 194

Chicken with Lemon, Capers, and Red Onions — 196

Golden Chicken and Taleggio Cutlets — 197

Parmigiano Chicken with Molten Provolone — 198

Pretzelized Chicken with
Cheddar Horseradish Sauce — 199

Miso-Walnut Chicken with Rainbow Swiss Chard — 200

Turkey Chopped Steak with Peas
and Pickled Onions — 201

Tangy Turkey and Snow Pea Stir-Fry — 202

Turkey Cutlets with Red Kidney Beans,
Garlic Relish, and Watercress — 203

Turkey, Broccoli, and Cheese Casserole — 206

Duck and Eggplant Flash-Fry — 207

**BEEF, PORK, AND LAMB MAIN DISHES** — 209

Sirloin Tips with Gorgonzola Mashed Potatoes — 210

Broiled Flat-Iron Steaks with
Pepper Jack Scalloped Potatoes — 211

Grilled Flank Steak with Shredded Carrots
and Pickled Ginger — 213

Beef and Broccoli-Coleslaw Stir-Fry — 214

Beef and Onion Flash-Fry — 215

Quick Steak, Pizza Man Style — 216

Beef Curry Sauté — 217

Roast Beef and Eggplant Alfredo — 220

Cheesy Roast Beef and Zucchini — 221

Roast Beef, Chestnuts, and Brussels Sprouts
in Consommé — 222

Beefy Shepherd's Pie — 223

Ground Beef with Refried Beans, Salsa,
and Grilled Zucchini — 224

Ground Beef with Salsa Verde, Radicchio,
and Sour Cream — 225

Corned Beef Brisket with Cabbage,
Potatoes, and Horseradish — 226

Veal Scaloppini in Artichoke Broth — 227

12 Eggs in a Pan — 230

Andouille Sausage Jambalaya
with Clams and Peas     **231**

Barbecue Kielbasa with Corn, Black Beans,
and Corn Muffins     **232**

Chorizo and Manchego Frittata
with Mesclun Salad     **233**

Hot Italian Sausage with Fresh Beans
and Beets     **234**

Chorizo, Smoked Mussel, and Okra Rice Pilaf     **235**

Kielbasa and Sauerkraut Stew     **236**

Boneless Pork Chops with Potato Pancakes
and Mustard Greens     **237**

Pork Scaloppini Stuffed with Cheddar     **238**

Pork and Zucchini Flash-Fry
with Black Bean Sauce     **239**

Sautéed Pork with Snow Peas, Walnuts,
and Beets     **240**

Stuffed Pork Chops with Boursin and Collards     **242**

Grilled Boneless Leg of Lamb
with Greek Yogurt Sauce     **244**

Grilled Lamb with Sweet-and-Sour
Cranberry Sauce     **245**

**DESSERTS**     **247**

Angel Food and Cherry Cake
with Ginger Cream     **248**

Apricot and Dried Cherry Pound Cake     **249**

Blueberry Pomegranate Consommé
with Whipped Crème Fraîche     **250**

Caramelized Banana Panini     **251**

Chocolate Phyllo with Blood Oranges
and Dulce de Leche Ice Cream     **254**

Cocoa Cookies with Black Raspberry Ice Cream
and Chocolate Fudge     **255**

Doughnuts and Hot Chocolate     **256**

Grilled Pineapple with Cocoa Foam     **257**

Instant Tiramisu with Raspberries     **258**

Crispy Wonton Wafers with Lemon Curd
and Strawberries     **259**

Pears in Phyllo Cups with Butter Pecan Ice Cream
and Caramel Sauce     **260**

Pretty Peach Melba     **261**

S'mores Tartlets     **262**

Warm Rice Pudding with Rum Raisin Ice Cream     **263**

Apple Pan Crumble     **264**

Baba au Rum     **265**

Butterscotch Chocolate Fondue with
Graham Crackers and Banana     **266**

Chocolate Cakes with Raspberries
and Nutella Mousse     **267**

Classic Cannoli     **268**

Crispy Golden Croissants with Pumpkin Cream
and Candied Ginger     **269**

Dutch Apples on Challah with
Maple-Walnut Sauce     **270**

Guava Tapioca with Macadamia Nuts     **271**

Fresh Oranges with Jack Daniel's and Yogurt     **272**

Pineapple French Toast     **273**

Croissants with Prunes and Armagnac     **274**

Thai Bling-Bling Soup     **275**

Warm Brownies with a Salty Peanut Sauce     **276**

**INDEX**     **277**

# Introduction

My hometown, or "hood," Jamaica, Queens, was a tough place to grow up in. It is the heart of the largest ethnic community in the country, and shots were fired almost daily. However, I was also blessed. In spite of the drugs and violence around me, in my house we lived the good life every day. My mom worked a full-time job as a public school lunch lady, but she made it home every night in time to prepare a fresh meal for us, and she still managed to do all the rest of the things moms do. My family cherished each other and the good times we had around the dinner table. My grandmother ran a farm and spoiled us rotten with the best eggs, tomatoes, and wine and abundant laughs. With my family, everyone was welcome, and there was always food for one more at our table. My neighbors were from all over the world, and they shared the flavors of their homelands with me. I got to try almost every flavor imaginable by the time I was fourteen. I didn't realize it then, but the legacy my family and my neighborhood gave me was an appreciation for people, a love of great flavors, and an education on how to share the good life with everyone, every day.

It was no coincidence that I ran headfirst into the world of cooking professionally at the age of fourteen. I was a prep cook at the New Hyde Park Inn in New York State when I decided to cook for a living. I remember the day I gave up high school wrestling to be a chef as clearly as I remember my first date.

The '60s and '70s were a time of tremendous social and cultural change in this country. The collective American palate began to change too; it was maturing, growing in sophistication by leaps and bounds.

At first, French chefs still dominated fine dining, but American chefs learned from their French masters and began to rock their own kitchens. They soon turned out highly personal and memorable meals as regularly as the French guys did.

This is where I came in. While working at the New Hyde Park Inn, I applied to the Culinary Institute of America. I was accepted and began there at the age of seventeen. After graduating, I went straight to Paris to find my way through the kitchens of France. I returned to New York City in 1988 and continued my training there, and I began a degree in business at Boston University in 1989. After graduation, New York City called again and I went to work with Gray Kunz in his four-star restaurant, Lespinasse. There my training and experiences really came together—and added up to more than the sum of their parts. By the time I was twenty-six, I'd graduated with honors from the Culinary Institute of America, earned a bachelor's degree from Boston University, and lived, worked, and eaten in Paris, Israel, Boston, and New York City. This evolution eventually landed me in my own very fancy New York City three-star kitchen and on the cover of *Gourmet* magazine. I was referred to as the "Flavor Guy," the chef who could bring flavors together as no one else could.

My first book, *Flavor,* won a James Beard Foundation Award, and I am very proud of it. Here, using the same principles as in *Flavor,* I want to bring intense, beautiful, and memorable flavors to people who simply don't have much time to cook. My goal now is to empower everyday cooks to grab their share of the good life by boiling down to its essence all my training, experience, and passion into a cookbook that can deliver fast, delicious food at home.

After a long career and many hours behind the stove, I have chosen to take a break from the day-to-day life of running a restaurant. In my new life, I've often found myself wondering, "Can a chef find happiness in New York City without a restaurant?" The answer is an emphatic "Yes!" Now I am *living* the good life every day instead of providing it for others. I have time to explore all those things I could never do before but worshipped from afar. I race motorcycles—fast ones—around a track with my knee to the ground, ski, and scuba dive; I even play guitar a few times a week. However, the most fun I have is when I cook for the people I love. I cook for myself almost every night now, instead of chomping down leftovers at 2 a.m. And I give dinner parties of my own. For me, the good life all started back in the days of my mother's home kitchen, and the home kitchen is where it will live forever.

In the 1980s, Pierre Franey's *60-Minute Gourmet* was a milestone in publishing for the home cook. More recently, *30 Minute Meals* by Rachel Ray made a huge splash. Now, I want to take America to the next level. I want 5 minutes to be the new 30 minutes. At first, I thought it could not be done; recipes made with 5 ingredients, cooked in 5 minutes, at no more than 5 dollars a serving? Insanity, right?

Wrong! It can be done, and in *Rocco's 5 Minute Flavor,* you'll learn how.

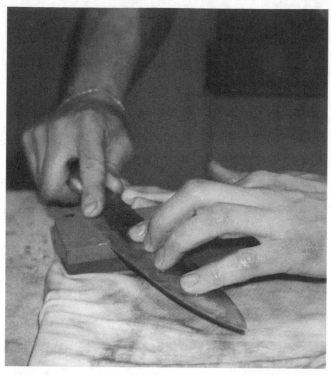

# What Have I Been Up To?

Over the past year or two, I have accomplished many things and made major changes in my life. I starred in NBC's *The Restaurant*; I opened and closed Rocco's 22nd Street. I published my second book, *Rocco's Italian American*; I sold Union Pacific, my three-star New York City restaurant; I became the host of *Food Talk with Rocco* on WOR radio; I wrote this book and began working on a new TV show; I created a line of cookware and a line of prepared foods; I cooked at the Oscars, the Grammys, and the Sundance Film Festival, and helped raise money for many charities, including Volunteers of America, Seeds of Peace, and the March of Dimes. I helped my mother through a near-fatal heart attack; happily, she survived and is doing great.

But as a chef, what was really new and special was that for the first time in my life, I was cooking like an everyday home cook. And I love it! Why do you think there is a Food Network, why are there so many markets and gourmet shops all over the place? It's all because we have finally learned that sharing food with your family and friends is totally what's up. The good life is right there in front of you; you just gotta grab it.

After cooking in restaurants every night for nearly twenty-five years, I've spent the last year cooking at home every night, and boy, have I learned a lot! I had always assumed that because I knew how to cook in a restaurant kitchen I knew how to cook in a home kitchen. But I didn't. The very first thing I learned was that I had a lot to learn. Then I learned that there wasn't enough time in a day to cook completely from scratch every night, that shopping for, searching out, selecting, purchasing, prepping, and cooking any more than 5 ingredients made my eyes glaze over. Sure, when I had suppliers deliver the finest ingredients to my kitchen and armies of prep cooks and chefs at my fingertips, many of my dishes had 10 or 20 ingredients in them. Well, that has all changed. Thrift is also now very important. Supermarket prices are manageable, but they require attention. Of course, I always knew that flavor is the thing. No dish, no matter how fast, how convenient, or how inexpensive, is worth its weight in dirt if it doesn't taste good.

My first book, *Flavor,* was all about creating dishes that boast great flavor combinations. My intention was to empower home cooks to discover the secrets of flavor. The aim of this book is no different. I did not compromise on flavor when I decided to cook each dish in 5 minutes with 5 ingredients for 5 dollars or less a person. Fast food is now fresh and flavorful food. No one has ever put speed, convenience, and thrift together with flavor the way you will be able to with *Rocco's 5 Minute Flavor.*

# HERE'S WHY 5 MINUTES IS THE NEW 30 MINUTES

America's collective palate has grown in leaps and bounds, and the purveyors of food for America's restaurants—and grocery stores—have responded with enthusiasm to their customers' evolving tastes. But it dawned on me that most Americans have been severely underusing these new resources. If you walk into any grocery store today, and do so with open eyes, you will find a treasure trove of prepared fresh foods, including precut vegetables and fruits; good canned soups and broths; roasted meats; condiments from around the world; and ready-to-go sauces and seasonings that, when used properly, can cut your cooking time down to, well, about 5 minutes. And if you use your newly found superpowers for good and take advantage of these shortcut foods, you can be a *5 Minute Flavor* hero, too.

There are aisles and aisles of things like cooked jarred beets; canned chicken stock; prepared artichokes; canned pears; Vietnamese chili sauce; sliced fresh portabella mushrooms; instant polenta; rice and couscous; diced red and green peppers and onions; cut and washed kale; canned peeled tomatoes; organic corn chowder; brownies; roasted chickens; freshly cooked roast beef—the list goes on and on. Unlike those in my two previous books, and most cookbooks in the marketplace, the dishes included here were inspired by the hundreds of high-quality prepared foods on supermarket shelves.

I chose these ingredients myself by painstakingly going through aisle after aisle and identifying, testing, tasting, and working them into recipes for this book. Only the ones I loved made it in. These foods can be found in the international section, the produce aisle, the frozen food case, the canned exotics section, the deli counter, even sometimes hanging on the shelf right next to the magazines at the checkout counter.

The ingredients for these recipes are broken down into two categories: 1) *pantry ingredients:* basics such as salt, pepper, sugar, vinegar, oil, butter, and flour that enable you to cook and season the dishes in this book; and 2) *main ingredients,* the five that make up each dish.

As pantry ingredients, water and these other basics are italicized in the ingredients list and are not counted as one of the five main ingredients in my recipes:

# 1. SALT & PEPPER
*sea salt and table salt, black and white pepper*

# 2. SUGAR
*granulated sugar, brown sugar, confectioners' sugar*

# 3. VINEGAR
*red wine, white wine, rice wine, sherry wine,
white vinegar, and cider vinegar*

# 4. FAT
*butter, olive oil, canola oil, soybean oil, grapeseed oil,
lard, chili oil, and garlic oil*

# 5. FLOUR
*all-purpose flour, corn flour, masa harina, and cornstarch*

Five minutes means *5 minutes.* Believe me when I tell you that we have tested all of these recipes over and over. We had friends and family, even strangers, test them. Let me tell you they are all, every one of them, designed to cook in 5 minutes. For real. If you take my upcoming sermon about high heat to heart, you will be a black belt in *5 minute flavor* on your first try. And if you don't, 7½ minutes isn't so bad, is it?

Prep time is not included in the 5 minutes, but I was careful to choose ingredients that require virtually no preparation since I wanted to stack the deck in your favor and empower you to be a successful *5 minute flavor* cook.

In addition to the many fresh ingredients called for in this book, here is a list of about a hundred shortcut foods I found to be inspiring, delicious, and good enough to use in these recipes:

## Cheese & Dairy Products
Boursin Cheese
Dannon's Crème de la Crème Vanilla Yogurt
Litehouse Avocado Dip
Parker's Farm Horseradish Cold Pack Cheese Food

## Fruits, Juices & Preserves
Musselman's Dutch Baked Apples
Pom Blueberry-Pomegranate Juice
Raspberry Polaner Pourable Fruit

## Beef, Chicken & Pork Products
Black Bear Beef Brisket
Black Bear Mini Beef Cocktail Franks
Black Bear Roast Beef
D'Artagnan Andouille Sausage
Hebrew National Hot Dogs
Nature's Reserve Boneless Ribeye Steak
Perdue Chicken

## Potatoes
Diner's Choice Country Style Mashed Potatoes
Diner's Choice Garlic Mashed Potatoes
Fresh From the Start Scallop Cut Potatoes
Fresh From the Start Cubed Bliss Potatoes
Fresh From the Start Cubed Golden Potatoes
Old Fashioned Kitchen Potato Pancake

## Produce
Black Bear Slow-Cooked Sweet Vidalia Onions
Cut 'N' Clean Collard Greens
Dole Classic Coleslaw Mix
Dole Classic Romaine Mix
Greenwood Harvard Beets
Greenwood Sweet and Sour Red Cabbage
Mann's Sunny Shores Broccoli Coleslaw
Ready Pac Sliced Peppers and Onions
Ready Pac Tri-Color Pepper Dice
Victoria Hot Dog Onions
Victoria Roasted Red Peppers

## Soups & Broths
Campbell's Cheddar Soup
Imagine Organic Butternut Squash Soup
Imagine Organic Creamy Sweet Corn Soup
Imagine Organic Portabella Mushroom Soup
Progresso Lentil Soup
Swanson Beef Broth
Swanson Chicken Broth

## Condiments, Dressings & Sauces
A-1 Steak Sauce
Buitoni Alfredo Sauce
Consorzio Garlic Oil
Dellalo Olive Bruschetta Topping
Gulden's Spicy Brown Mustard
Heinz Home-Style Savory Beef Gravy
Hellmann's Dijonnaise
Ken's Creamy Caesar Dressing
Steve and Ed's Buffalo Wing Sauce
Stubbs Original Barbecue Sauce
Victoria Fra Diavolo Sauce
Victoria Marinara Sauce

## Asian Products
General Tso's Sauce
House of Tsang Bangkok Padang Peanut Sauce
House of Tsang Classic Stir-Fry Sauce
House of Tsang Hibachi Grill Sweet Ginger Sesame Sauce

House of Tsang Mongolian Fire Oil
Kame Black Bean Sauce
Kame Coconut Curry Marinade
Maggi Seasoning
Mikee Garlic Rib Sauce
Mikee Garlic Stir-Fry and Rib Sauce
Mikee Sesame Teriyaki Sauce
S&M Wasabi Paste
Taste of Thai Peanut Satay Sauce
Thai Kitchen Coconut Ginger Soup
Thai Kitchen Lemongrass and Chile Soup Mix
Thai Kitchen Original Pad Thai Sauce

## Indian Products
Patak's Hot Curry Paste
Patak's Medium Garlic Relish
Patak's Sweet Mango Chutney
Patak's Tangy Lemon and Cilantro Cooking Sauce

## Mexican Products
Frontera's Salsa Verde
Goya Recaito
Goya Sofrito
Old El Paso Refried Beans
Santa Barbara Hot Salsa
Tostitos Salsa con Queso

## Breadsticks, Crackers & Nuts
Cheez-It
Mauna Loa Macadamia Pieces
Stella D'Oro Sesame Breadsticks

## Couscous, Stuffing, Pasta & Flour
Delverde Pasta
Near East Couscous Mix
Stovetop Turkey Stuffing Mix
Wondra Flour

## Cookies & Doughnuts
Archway Dutch Cocoa Cookies
Entenmann's Donuts Shoppe Powdered
Sugar Donuts
Krispy Kreme Doughnuts

## Baking Products
Coco Lopez Cream of Coconut
Keebler Mini Graham Cracker Pie Crusts
La Rosa Cannoli Shells

## Puddings, Frozen Desserts & Dessert Sauces
Ben and Jerry's Butter Pecan Ice Cream
Ciao Bella Mango Sorbet
Flav-O-Ice
Häagen-Dazs Dulce de Leche Ice Cream
Häagen-Dazs Peaches and Cream Ice Cream
Häagen-Dazs Pineapple Coconut Ice Cream
Jell-O Gelatin Snacks
Kozy Shack Rice Pudding
Kozy Shack Tapioca Pudding
Silver Palate Very Fudge Sauce
Stonewall Espresso Mocha Sauce
Sharon's Passion Fruit Sorbet

## Miscellaneous Frozen Products
McKenzie's Southland Butternut Squash Puree
Northern Chef Frozen Clams on the Half-Shell
Pepperidge Farms Puff Pastry

# MOST OF US DON'T HAVE THE LUXURY OF OWNING A VIKING RANGE

I've had a few epiphanies lately. Among them was the discovery that at home, almost nobody has enough BTUs (British Thermal Units—it's the way we measure heat) to cook quickly. You have seen the burning-hot woks in the kitchens of Chinese restaurants and the huge ranges and broilers in professional kitchens, and in the kitchens of the friends you envy for cooking on a Viking range. Such cooks possess a fire-breathing dragon, a home range with giant muscular burners, a blinding broiler, and a powerful convection oven. Well, I don't own one and I am assuming you don't either.

Think about this: An average home range draws 10,000 BTUs per burner. In my restaurants, I cooked on ranges that drew 100,000 BTUs—now that's cooking with gas! When I left the restaurants, I didn't run out and buy a Viking range for my home. Instead, I figured out how to compensate. High heat is the key! If I say it a thousand times, it won't be too much. You need to cook these dishes with high heat. Now when I say high heat, here is what I mean: Put a pan on a hot burner and go watch *The Godfather, then* come back and start cooking. Give that pan time to really heat up! The best way to capture high heat on your home stoves is to do exactly that: capture it. While the home range doesn't have the per-minute output of a professional kitchen, it does have the unlimited heat of a restaurant kitchen. Retaining that heat long enough to keep your water boiling, your deep-fat frying oil hot, and your pan sizzling till the end is easy. All you need is the right equipment and the courage to get your equipment hot enough for super-fast cooking. This means five pieces of cookware and appliances that I am sure all of you own and/or can afford to buy immediately.

# 1. Sauté pan

The first thing you need is a large sauté pan with high sides, like a 5-quart chicken fryer. Make sure it has at least a 1/2-inch-thick clad bottom, or choose a cast-iron pan, such as one from Lodge, with or without porcelain, or a 5-quart cast-iron pan with porcelain enamel from a maker such as Le Creuset. Circulon makes a heavy cast-aluminum pan that does the trick as well. These pans range from $25 to $125, and any one of them will work.

# 2. Stovetop grill pan

The next thing you'll need is a stovetop grill pan. Again, Lodge, Le Creuset, and Circulon all make great ones. Again, a heavy and thick clad bottom for retaining heat is a must. And be sure it is large enough to hold four portions, because every recipe in this book is for four people.

# 3. A 6- to 8-quart stockpot/ pasta pot

This is essential for boiling water and deep-fat frying.

# 4. Broiler

I have rediscovered the power of the oven broiler. Again, while not as hot as a professional kitchen broiler, it has unlimited output: Just turn it on and give it time to let the heat build.

# 5. Microwave oven

I have also discovered that the microwave oven can be a terrific partner in the quest for 5 minute flavor.

# While we are talking, some of my fave appliances are:

## Immersion blender

It makes blending so easy and cleanup silly.

## Food processor

If you want speed in the kitchen, this is your best friend.

## Fondue pot

I call for a fondue pot for my fondue recipes. Although any pot with high sides will do, a fondue set is a great investment, particularly for making Swiss fondue, which is a hot pot of oil placed in the center of the table, letting guests cook their own bite-size pieces of meat, poultry, or fish.

# Here are a few of my favorite tips:

You can reduce a pan's heat if it's too hot before cooking by adding water to it. Once it's cooled a bit, you just throw the water in the sink, wipe the pan dry, and proceed.

Properly frying foods is a great way to save time and add flavor. As long as the heat is high enough, fried foods will not become fat sponges. Deep-frying is also a great way to allow your guests to participate. I love Swiss fondue—you provide the food and the forks or skewers, and your guests do the rest.

Grinding whole spices in a small electric coffee grinder is a great way to punch up flavor. It smells good too.

**ROCCO'S 5 MINUTE FLAVOR**

Who knew you didn't have to spend loads of money to make great food at home? In my career as a professional chef, I have spent twenty to fifty dollars, sometimes even hundreds of dollars, *per person* on ingredients, to make dishes such as White Truffle Risotto with Gulf Shrimp or Kobe Beef with Galangal-Glazed Ramps. Many of those ingredients are both rare and exciting to work with, for sure. But when you are shopping to cook at home, you can't afford to spend half your weekly salary on food. Yet it turns out the last restraint I put on myself for this book—dishes for under 5 dollars a portion—was easy. Fresh food is much less expensive than take-out or prepackaged meals, and by creating dishes that usually have two to four fresh ingredients and only one or two prepared ingredients, I was able to get the best of both worlds into these recipes. Most of the dishes are well under 5 dollars per person; even those that call for luxury ingredients such as crab and lobster never surpass the 5-dollar mark.

# Menus

I broke the recipes down into the smallest, most specific categories I could think of, because I wanted to make it easy for you to develop 2-, 3-, even 4-course menus from them. Here are some of my favorite menus, organized by season or occasion.

## Vegetarian
*This is a meatless menu that isn't just grilled vegetables or an omelet.*

Warm Artichoke Parmigiano Dip
Eggplant Parmigiano
Butterscotch Chocolate Fondue with Graham Crackers and Banana

## Holiday Feast
*I had Christmas in mind when I created this menu, but it would be just as suitable for Thanksgiving, New Year's, or any other cold-weather family gathering.*

Salmon and Sesame Swiss Fondue
Prosciutto, Parmigiano, Pimiento, and Arugula Salad
Grilled Lamb with Sweet-and-Sour Cranberry Sauce
Classic Cannoli

## Super Bowl Sunday
*This feast makes for great eating and always wins big at my Super Bowl parties. Serve as a buffet with plenty of beer.*

Pigs in a Blanket Swiss Fondue
Mushroom Quesadillas
Fresh Fast Guacamole
Buffalo Chicken Tenders with Celery and Blue Cheese Salad
Roast Beef Wrap with Garlic Relish

## Pants Too Tight
*We all know the feeling; these low-fat dishes won't make them any tighter.*

Grilled Asparagus and Oyster Mushrooms with Pecorino Cheese

Salmon with Shiitake Mushrooms in Ginger-Soy Broth
Guava Tapioca with Macadamia Nuts

## Mother's Day

*For a light, elegant spring brunch or dinner.*

Fennel-Seared Chicken Livers with
Watercress and Oranges
Turkey, Broccoli, and Cheese Casserole
Baba au Rum

## Dead-of-Winter Feast

*From start to finish, this meal is a perfect excuse
to go nowhere on an inhumanely cold February day.*

Clams Oreganata
Grilled Stuffed Veal with Basil and Provolone
Roast Beef Borscht
Warm Rice Pudding with Rum Raisin Ice Cream

## Valentine's Day

*A very romantic, red-hued meal.*

Firecracker Shrimp
Quick Steak, Pizza Man Style
Thai Bling-Bling Soup

## Blowout Celebration

*A long-awaited promotion, thirtieth birthday,
or a windfall from a court ruling. . . .
Whatever the event, this pull-out-all-the-stops
menu is perfect for celebrating.*

Duck Swiss Fondue
Veal Scallopini in Artichoke Broth
Instant Tiramisu with Raspberries

## Meeting the In-Laws

*The occasion is stressful enough as it is!
Go with safe dishes that are easy to make
and universally liked.*

Fried Calamari and Artichokes with Hummus
Chicken and Chopped Salad
Broiled Flat-Iron Steaks with Pepper Jack
Scalloped Potatoes
Donuts and Hot Chocolate

## New House

*Where the heck is the food processor? Unpack the
boxes later. You can make everything on this menu
with a few pans, a bowl, and a baking sheet.*

Shrimp Swiss Fondue with Arrabbiata Dipping Sauce
Tangy Turkey and Snow Pea Stir-Fry
Warm Brownies with Salty Peanut Sauce

## Too Hot to Cook

*It's 97 degrees outside—next to the stove is the last
place you want to be. Keep cool with this light menu
of no-cook/quick-cook summer dishes.*

Chilled Cucumber Soup with Smoked Salmon
and Crème Fraîche
Peanut Chicken and Radicchio Salad
Blueberry Pomegranate Consommé with
Whipped Crème Fraîche

## A Midsummer's Night Menu

*Here are foods that are great in the summer,
a fabulous picnic-under-the-stars menu.*

Shrimp Salad with Red Onion, Mango, and Cilantro
Pierogi with Ham, Dandelion Greens, and Sour Cream
Mustard Sauce
Pretty Peach Melba

## Beach House Blast

*This spread features some of the foods you're
likely to come by on the way to the shore: roadside
produce-stand fare like corn, tomatoes, and
apricots, plus fish and shellfish.*

Tomato and Mozzarella Salad
Sautéed Scallops with Pickled Ginger Red Cabbage
Apricot and Dried Cherry Pound Cake

## Make Ahead

*Make these dishes ahead and reheat
(if necessary) in a flash.*

Mushroom Soup with Boursin Croutons
Avocado Salad with Red Onion and Feta
Andouille Sausage Jambalaya with Clams and Peas
Apple Pan Crumble

# Cocktail Party Spread

*Designed to feed four, these recipes can easily double or triple as your RSVPs roll in.*

Tuna Tempura Swiss Fondue with Wasabi Soy
Duck Swiss Fondue
Garlicky Lemon Shrimp
Puffy Chicken with Green Curry Basil Sauce
Toasted Hot Dog Reuben
Smoked Salmon and Swiss Cheese Panini

# Autumn Harvest

*The September shift to cooler weather never fails to reinvigorate our desire to cook. Good thing, since autumn is an agriculturally rich season in all parts of the country.*

Stracciatella
Miso-Walnut Chicken with Rainbow Swiss Chard
Dutch Apples on Challah with Maple-Walnut Sauce

# Fungus Extravaganza

*Indulge your love of mushrooms. Some of us just can't get enough of these earthy flavors.*

Rich Mushroom Bouillon
Mushroom and Red Onion Burgers
S'mores Tartlets

# For Cheese Lovers

*Want to try several cheeses in one meal? As an alternative to the traditional cheese tray, consider serving courses of dishes with cheese.*

Mushroom Quesadillas
Pear and Stilton Salad
Golden Chicken and Taleggio Cutlets
Chocolate Phyllo with Blood Oranges and
Dulce de Leche Ice Cream

# Designed to Impress

*The "Ooh! Ah! Ohhh!" quotient is high.*
*Perfect for entertaining royalty or closing a deal.*

See-Thru Scallops with Lemon Brown Butter
and Celery Leaves
Beef Shabu-Shabu with Watercress
Savory Seafood Stew
Croissants with Prunes and Armagnac

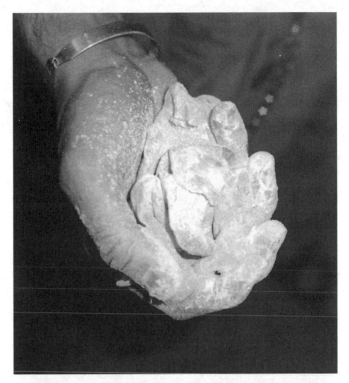

# Appetizers

# FRESH FAST GUACAMOLE

**Number of Servings: 4**  *Estimated Cost: $9.50*

½ **jalapeño pepper, sliced**
½ **red onion, cut into large chunks**
**1 cup fresh tightly packed cilantro leaves**
**3 large ripe avocados, pitted and peeled**
*Salt and freshly ground black pepper*
**Tortilla chips**

**1.** Combine the jalapeño pepper, red onion, and cilantro in the bowl of a food processor; pulse to chop fine. Or combine on a cutting board and finely chop with a sharp knife.

**2.** In a medium bowl, mash the avocados. Add the chopped onion mixture and mix thoroughly. Season with salt and pepper.

**3.** Serve immediately, with chips. Or allow to chill for 1 hour in the refrigerator before serving; cover the surface of the guacamole directly with plastic wrap to keep it from discoloring.

# WARM ARTICHOKE PARMIGIANO DIP

**Number of Servings: 4**  *Estimated Cost: $7*

1 (14-ounce) can artichoke hearts, drained and finely chopped
¾ cup reduced-fat mayonnaise
1 cup grated Parmigiano-Reggiano cheese
2 large cloves garlic, finely chopped or put through a garlic press
2 tablespoons chopped fresh basil

**1.** In a medium bowl, combine all the ingredients and mix well. Spread the mixture evenly in a 7 x 7-inch baking dish.

**2.** Microwave for 4 to 5 minutes, stirring twice to make sure the dip is heating evenly. Serve hot, with pita chips or your favorite chips or crackers.

# GRILLED ASPARAGUS AND OYSTER MUSHROOMS WITH PECORINO CHEESE

**Number of Servings: 4** *Estimated Cost: $20*

**2 lemons**
**2 bunches pencil-thin asparagus, tough ends trimmed**
**11 ounces oyster mushrooms, cut into small clusters**
*⅔ cup extra virgin olive oil*
*Salt and freshly ground black pepper*
**⅓ cup chopped fresh chives**
**An 8-ounce wedge pecorino cheese**

**1.** Heat a large grill pan until very hot.

**2.** Meanwhile, grate the zest from both lemons. Squeeze the juice from 1½ lemons.

**3.** In a large shallow bowl, toss the asparagus and mushrooms with ⅓ cup of the oil to coat well. Season with salt and pepper. Grill the asparagus and mushrooms, turning often to ensure even coloring, until cooked through and slightly charred. Remove from the grill as the asparagus and mushrooms are done.

**4.** Meanwhile, combine the lemon zest, lemon juice, chives, and the remaining ⅓ cup oil.

**5.** Divide the asparagus and mushrooms among four plates and drizzle the sauce liberally on top. With a vegetable peeler, slice curls of pecorino cheese on top. Serve.

# MUSHROOM QUESADILLAS

**Number of Servings: 4**  *Estimated Cost: $10.75*

**4 (12-inch) flour tortillas**
**2½ cups grated sharp cheddar cheese**
**¼ cup pickled sliced jalapeños, drained and chopped**
**2 cups sliced shiitake mushrooms**
*2 tablespoons corn oil*
**1 cup sour cream**

**1.** Heat two medium nonstick sauté pans over medium heat.

**2.** Meanwhile, place 2 of the tortillas on a work surface. Sprinkle the cheese, jalapeños, and mushrooms evenly over them. Top each tortilla with another tortilla and press down gently.

**3.** Add 1 tablespoon of the oil to each sauté pan. Carefully place 1 of the quesadillas in each pan. Cook for about 2 minutes, or until golden brown on the bottom. Use tongs to carefully flip both quesadillas, and cook for another 2 minutes, or until the cheese is melted and they are golden brown on the second side. Adjust the heat if necessary to keep them from scorching. Transfer the quesadillas to a cutting board and let stand for about 1 minute.

**4.** Slice each quesadilla into 8 wedges. Serve with the sour cream.

# NEW-STYLE TUNA SASHIMI

**Number of Servings: 4**  *Estimated Cost: $17.50*

¾ to 1 pound sushi-quality tuna, very thinly sliced
1 tablespoon sesame seeds
*Salt*
½ cup radishes cut into thin strips
1 small bunch scallions, thinly sliced on the diagonal
½ cup plus 1 tablespoon ponzu sauce
*2 tablespoons hot chili oil*

**1.** Divide the tuna into 4 portions and arrange it on four large plates (the "faces" of the plates should be about 7 to 8 inches in diameter), covering them completely and overlapping the tuna slices only slightly as necessary.

**2.** Sprinkle the sesame seeds over the tuna and lightly season with salt.

**3.** Toss together the radishes and scallions in a small bowl. Set aside.

**4.** Combine the ponzu sauce and chili oil in a small saucepan and bring to a boil.

**5.** Drizzle the chili oil mixture evenly over the tuna to "cook" it. Scatter the radishes and scallions over the tuna, and serve immediately.

# CREAMY LEMON SHRIMP SALAD WITH CUCUMBERS AND WATERCRESS

**Number of Servings: 4** *Estimated Cost: $18.50*

**5 lemons**
**¾ cup mayonnaise**
**¼ pound cooked peeled shrimp, split in half**
**1⅔ cups diced cucumber**
*Salt and freshly ground black pepper*
**1 bunch (about 2½ cups) watercress, trimmed and cleaned**

**1.** Grate the zest from 4 of the lemons. Put the zest in a medium bowl and squeeze the juice from one of the zested lemons into the bowl. Add the mayonnaise and mix well.

**2.** Add the shrimp and cucumbers to the lemon mayonnaise and toss well to coat. Season with salt and pepper.

**3.** Make a bed of watercress in the center of each of four plates. Pile the shrimp on top of the watercress. Grate the zest of the remaining lemon over the salads, and serve.

# FRIED CALAMARI AND ARTICHOKES WITH HUMMUS DIPPING SAUCE

**Number of Servings: 4**  *Estimated Cost: $18.50*

*3 quarts canola oil*
**1½ cups prepared hummus**
**6 tablespoons olive paste**
*½ cup water*
**3 tablespoons chopped fresh rosemary**
*Flour for dredging*
*Salt and freshly ground black pepper*
**1¼ pounds squid, cleaned and thinly sliced**
**1 (14-ounce) can quartered artichoke hearts, drained**

**1.** Heat the oil in a large pot until hot but not smoking, about 375 degrees.

**2.** In a medium bowl, mix the hummus, olive paste, water, and rosemary.

**3.** Spread the flour on a plate and season with salt and pepper. Dredge the calamari and artichoke quarters in the flour. Fry until crispy and golden, about 5 minutes. Drain well on paper towels. Season the calamari with salt and pepper.

**4.** Serve the calamari and artichokes with small bowls of the dipping sauce alongside.

# CLAMS OREGANATA

**Number of Servings: 4**  *Estimated Cost: $12.50*

*9 tablespoons butter, melted*
**3 cloves garlic, chopped**
**3 tablespoons fresh lemon juice**
**1 (¾ ounce) package fresh oregano, leaves picked and finely chopped**
**2 cups dried bread crumbs**
*Salt and freshly ground black pepper*
**1½ pounds frozen clams on the half-shell**

**1.** Preheat the oven to 500 degrees.

**2.** Combine the butter, garlic, lemon juice, oregano, and bread crumbs in a medium bowl. Season with salt and pepper.

**3.** Lay the clams on a baking sheet lined with foil. Pile some of the bread crumb mixture on each clam, covering the entire surface.

**4.** Bake for 3½ minutes; you should be able to hear the clams sizzling when you open the oven. Turn on the oven broiler and continue to cook until the bread crumbs have crisped and turned a deep golden brown. Serve immediately.

# MUSSELS WITH HUMMUS BROTH AND CRUSTY ITALIAN BREAD

**Number of Servings: 4**  *Estimated Cost: $12*

**4 large slices Italian sourdough bread**
**6 garlic cloves, 4 chopped, 2 peeled but left whole**
*2 tablespoons extra virgin olive oil*
*Salt and freshly ground black pepper*
*1 tablespoon hot chili oil*
**½ cup prepared hummus**
**⅔ cup dry white wine**
*½ cup water*
**2 pounds mussels, scrubbed and debearded**

**1.** Heat a grill pan until very hot.

**2.** Rub the bread on both sides with the 2 whole garlic cloves and brush both sides with the olive oil and season with salt and pepper. Grill, turning once, until lightly charred.

**3.** Meanwhile, heat a very large straight-sided sauté pan until very hot. Add the chili oil. Immediately add the chopped garlic and cook, stirring, until aromatic and golden brown. Add the hummus, then whisk in the wine and water; bring to a boil.

**4.** Add the mussels, cover, and steam for about 1½ minutes, until they open.

**5.** Ladle the mussels and broth into bowls, and serve the bread alongside for dipping.

# FIRECRACKER SHRIMP

**Number of Servings: 4**  *Estimated Cost: $19*

*3 quarts canola oil*
**1 (10-ounce) jar mayonnaise, chilled**
**3 tablespoons Vietnamese chili garlic sauce**
*Flour for dredging*
*Salt and freshly ground black pepper*
**3 eggs**
**1 cup bread crumbs**
**1½ pounds jumbo tiger shrimp, peeled and deveined**

**1.** In a large pot, heat the oil to 400 degrees.

**2.** Meanwhile, in a medium bowl, mix together the mayonnaise and chili sauce. Set aside.

**3.** Spread the flour on a plate and season with salt and pepper. Lightly beat the eggs in a shallow bowl. Spread the bread crumbs on another plate. Dredge the shrimp in the flour, then coat in the eggs, and, finally, dredge thoroughly in the bread crumbs.

**4.** Submerge the shrimp in the oil and fry until golden brown and cooked through, about 2 minutes. Drain on paper towels and season with salt and pepper. Serve immediately, with the chili mayonnaise.

# GARLICKY LEMON SHRIMP

**Number of Servings: 4**  *Estimated Cost: $16.50*

**1 pound medium shrimp (36 to 40 count), peeled and deveined**
**3 tablespoons fresh lemon juice**
*¼ cup extra virgin olive oil*
**3 cloves garlic, finely chopped**
*Salt and freshly ground black pepper*
**½ cup grated Parmigiano-Reggiano cheese**
**¾ cup bread crumbs**

**1.** Preheat the oven to 500 degrees.

**2.** In a medium bowl, toss the shrimp with the lemon juice, olive oil, and garlic. Season well with salt and pepper. Add the cheese and bread crumbs and toss well to coat the shrimp evenly.

**3.** Spread the shrimp on a baking sheet in a single layer. Bake for 5 minutes, or until golden brown and cooked through. Serve immediately.

# SEE-THRU SCALLOPS WITH LEMON BROWN BUTTER AND CELERY LEAVES

**Number of Servings: 4**  *Estimated Cost: $18.75*

**8 ounces very fresh large sea scallops, tough side muscle removed, at room temperature**
*Salt and freshly ground black pepper*
**3 tablespoons chopped fresh chives**
**½ cup pale green celery leaves (from the heart of the celery)**
*7 tablespoons unsalted butter*
**¼ cup fresh lemon juice, or to taste**

**1.** With a very sharp knife, slice the scallops horizontally (about ⅛ inch thick). Arrange the scallops in a single layer on a medium serving plate, covering it completely. Season lightly with salt and pepper. Scatter the chives and celery leaves evenly over the scallops. Set aside.

**2.** In a small sauté pan, heat the butter over medium heat until it is brown and very fragrant. Turn off the heat and whisk in the lemon juice. (It should look somewhat creamy, not oily.) Season the sauce with salt and pepper, and taste—it should be very lemony; add more lemon juice if necessary.

**3.** Spoon the sauce liberally over the scallops, and serve immediately.

# FENNEL-SEARED CHICKEN LIVERS WITH WATERCRESS AND ORANGES

**Number of Servings: 4** *Estimated Cost: $9.50*

**4 navel oranges**
*⅓ cup plus 1 tablespoon olive oil*
*⅓ cup flour*
**2 tablespoons fennel seeds, crushed**
**1¼ pounds chicken livers, trimmed and patted dry**
*Salt and freshly ground black pepper*
*3 tablespoons sherry vinegar*
*1 teaspoon sugar*
**2 small bunches watercress, trimmed and washed**

**1.** With a sharp knife, remove the skin and white pith from the oranges. Cut the oranges into thin slices, and set aside.

**2.** In a large sauté pan, heat ⅓ cup oil until very hot. Mix together the flour and fennel seeds on a plate. Season the chicken livers with salt and pepper and dredge in the flour-fennel mixture. Sauté, turning once, until deep golden brown on both sides, about 2 to 3 minutes; be careful not to overcook. Remove from the pan and set aside.

**3.** Off the heat, add the remaining 1 tablespoon oil, the sherry vinegar, and sugar to the pan, then add the oranges and toss to coat. Transfer to a large bowl, add the watercress and chicken livers, and toss gently. Season with salt and pepper if necessary.

**4.** Divide the salad among four plates, and serve immediately.

# PUFFY CHICKEN WITH GREEN CURRY BASIL SAUCE

**Number of Servings: 4**  *Estimated Cost: $19*

*3 quarts canola oil*
**1 (8.8-ounce) package thin rice noodles**
**1½ pounds chicken tenders, cut lengthwise in half**
*Salt and freshly ground black pepper*
**1 (8.45-ounce) bottle coconut curry marinade**
**1 tablespoon Thai green curry paste**
**¼ cup chopped fresh basil**

**1.** In a large pot, heat the oil to 400 degrees.

**2.** Meanwhile, with kitchen shears or a sharp knife, cut the rice noodles into ½-inch pieces. Coat the chicken tenders with the noodles, pressing the noodles onto the chicken.

**3.** Fry the chicken, in batches if necessary, for about 1 minute, or until the noodles are puffy and crisp and the chicken is cooked through. Drain on paper towels, and season with salt and pepper.

**4.** While the tenders are cooking, heat the coconut curry marinade and green curry paste in a small saucepan. Add the basil.

**5.** Serve the chicken tenders with the dipping sauce alongside.

# GRILLED STUFFED VEAL WITH BASIL AND PROVOLONE

**Number of Servings: 4** *Estimated Cost: $17.25*

**4 very thin veal cutlets (about 4 ounces each)**
**8 thin slices sharp provolone**
**16 large fresh basil leaves**
**3 ounces sliced prosciutto**
**2 cloves garlic, chopped**
*3 tablespoons extra virgin olive oil*
*Salt and freshly ground black pepper*

**1.** Heat a large grill pan until very hot.

**2.** Set the veal cutlets on a work surface. Place 1 slice of cheese on the bottom half of each cutlet. Top each one with one-quarter of the prosciutto, 4 basil leaves, and another slice of cheese, then fold the top half of the cutlet over to cover. Press down on each "package" firmly; if desired, thread a toothpick through each cutlet to keep it closed.

**3.** Combine the garlic and olive oil, and rub the stuffed veal packages generously with this mixture. Season the veal liberally with salt and pepper. Grill for about 2 minutes on each side, or until the veal is just cooked through and the cheese has melted. Serve immediately.

# Fondues

# SHARP CHEDDAR AND BEER FONDUE WITH WARM PRETZELS

**Number of Servings: 4**  *Estimated Cost: $8.25*

**4 large frozen pretzels**
**½ cup strong dark beer**
**2 tablespoons finely chopped red onion**
*2 teaspoons cornstarch*
**½ pound extra-sharp cheddar cheese, shredded**
*Salt and freshly ground black pepper*

**1.** Cook the pretzels in an oven or toaster oven according to the package instructions. Keep warm.

**2.** Meanwhile, whisk together the beer, red onion, and cornstarch in a small saucepan. Bring to a boil, whisking constantly, and boil, whisking, until slightly thickened. Gradually whisk in the cheese, whisking until the cheese is completely melted and the fondue is smooth. Season with salt and pepper.

**3.** Serve the fondue with the warm pretzels for dipping.

# MUSHROOM FONDUE

**Number of Servings: 4**  *Estimated Cost: $13*

½ **cup dry white wine**
¼ *cup water*
½ **pound Gruyère cheese, grated**
*2 teaspoons cornstarch*
**1 cup very thinly sliced shiitake mushrooms**
**2 tablespoons chopped fresh tarragon**
*Salt and freshly ground black pepper*
**1 loaf Italian or French bread, cut into 1-inch cubes**

**1.** In a fondue pot or saucepan, bring the wine and water to a simmer over medium heat.

**2.** Meanwhile, in a medium bowl, toss the cheese with cornstarch to coat evenly.

**3.** Add one-third of the cheese mixture to the simmering wine mixture and stir with a whisk until completely melted. Add the remaining cheese in 2 batches, whisking until it is completely melted and the fondue is bubbling. Turn the heat to low and add the mushrooms and tarragon. Stir until heated through. Season with salt and pepper to taste. Check the fondue for consistency: if you prefer a thinner fondue, add a few tablespoons of water and stir vigorously until smooth; if you prefer it thicker, cook a bit longer.

**4.** Serve the fondue with the bread cubes and fondue forks. You could serve a small cup of Kirschwasser (cherry brandy) alongside for your guests to dip their bread into before dipping into the fondue.

# SALMON AND SESAME SWISS FONDUE

**Number of Servings: 4**  *Estimated Cost: $15.75*

*5 cups canola oil*
**½ cup sesame seeds**
**1 pound skinless salmon fillet, cut into 1- to 1½-inch cubes**
*Salt and freshly ground black pepper*
**⅔ cup tamari soy sauce**
**3 tablespoons fresh lemon juice**
*1 tablespoon sugar*
*2 teaspoons chili oil*

**1.** In a 4-quart fondue pot or saucepan, heat the canola oil to 400 degrees.

**2.** Meanwhile, put the sesame seeds in a shallow bowl. Season the salmon with salt and pepper and coat with the sesame seeds. Arrange on a platter.

**3.** For the dipping sauce, mix together the tamari, lemon juice, sugar, and chili oil. Place in a small serving bowl and serve alongside the salmon with skewers or fondue forks.

**4.** Invite your guests to skewer the salmon and cook in the hot oil for about 1 minute for medium-rare; allow to cool briefly, then dip into the sauce before eating.

# TUNA TEMPURA SWISS FONDUE WITH WASABI SOY

**Number of Servings: 4**  *Estimated Cost: $20*

*5 cups canola oil*
**1¼ pounds tuna, cut into 1- to 1¼-inch cubes**
**1½ cups packaged tempura mix**
*1¼ cups ice-cold water*
**½ cup tamari soy sauce**
**1 tablespoon wasabi paste**

**1.** In a 4-quart fondue pot or saucepan, heat the oil to 400 degrees.

**2.** Meanwhile, arrange the tuna on a serving platter.

**3.** To make the tempura batter, in a medium bowl, gradually add the tempura mix to the water, whisking constantly. Set the batter over a larger bowl of ice.

**4.** To make the dipping sauce, mix the soy sauce and wasabi together in a small serving bowl.

**5.** Using skewers or fondue forks, invite your guests to skewer the tuna and dip it into the tempura batter, then immediately into the hot oil; cook for 30 seconds for rare. Serve with the dipping sauce.

# SHRIMP SWISS FONDUE WITH ARRABBIATA DIPPING SAUCE

**Number of Servings: 4**  *Estimated Cost: $14.50*

*6 cups canola oil*
**1 pound shrimp (36 to 40 count), peeled and deveined**
*Salt and freshly ground black pepper*
**2 cups buttermilk**
*2 cups flour*
**2 cups prepared Fra Diavolo Sauce**
**¼ teaspoon red pepper flakes**

**1.** In a 4-quart fondue pot or saucepan, heat the oil to 400 degrees.

**2.** Meanwhile, season the shrimp well with salt and pepper. Soak in the buttermilk for 2 minutes, then drain in a colander and immediately dredge in the flour. Shake off the excess flour and arrange the shrimp on a platter.

**3.** Combine the sauce and red pepper flakes and heat in a microwave or saucepan until very hot. Transfer to a serving bowl.

**4.** Using skewers or fondue forks, invite guests to skewer the shrimp and cook in the hot oil for about 1½ minutes. Serve with the sauce for dipping.

# CHICKEN SWISS FONDUE WITH DIJON SOUR CREAM AND HUMMUS

**Number of Servings: 4** *Estimated Cost: $14*

*6 cups canola oil*
**½ cup plus 2 tablespoons sour cream**
**½ cup plus 2 tablespoons Dijon mustard**
**1 cup prepared scallion hummus**
*3 tablespoons water*
**1¼ pounds chicken tenders, cut crosswise in half**
*Salt and freshly ground black pepper*
*2 cups corn flour or masa harina*

**1.** In a 4-quart fondue pot or saucepan, heat the oil to 400 degrees.

**2.** Meanwhile, mix together the sour cream and mustard, and transfer to a small serving bowl. Mix together the hummus and water and transfer to another serving bowl. Set aside.

**3.** Season the chicken tenders with salt and pepper and dredge in the corn flour. Arrange the chicken on a platter.

**4.** Using skewers or fondue forks, invite your guests to skewer the chicken and dip in the hot oil for about 1 minute to cook through. Cool slightly before eating. Serve with the hummus and Dijon sour cream for dipping.

# DUCK SWISS FONDUE

**Number of Servings: 4**  *Estimated Cost: $18.75*

*5 cups canola oil*
**3 eggs**
**2½ cups bread crumbs**
**1 duck (about 6 pounds), skin removed, cut into 1-inch chunks**
**(ask your butcher to cut the duck apart for you)**
*Salt and freshly ground black pepper*
**1 cup prepared duck sauce**
**¼ cup Chinese mustard**

**1.** In a 4-quart fondue pot or saucepan, heat the oil to 400 degrees.

**2.** Meanwhile, beat the eggs in a shallow bowl. Spread the bread crumbs on a plate. Season the duck with salt and pepper. Dip in the egg, then coat in the bread crumbs. Arrange on a platter.

**3.** Mix the duck sauce and mustard, and transfer to a small serving bowl.

**4.** Invite your guests to skewer the duck and cook in the hot oil for 45 seconds to 1 minute; allow to cool slightly before dipping in the sauce.

# BEEF SWISS FONDUE WITH THREE SAUCES

**Number of Servings: 4**  *Estimated Cost: $19.50*

6 cups canola oil
**8 sesame bread sticks**
**1¼ pounds boneless beef shell steaks, cut into 1-inch chunks**
*Salt and freshly ground black pepper*
**1 cup salsa con queso**
**1 cup prepared hot dog onions**
**1 cup chow-chow relish**

**1.** In a 4-quart fondue pot or saucepan, heat the oil to 400 degrees.

**2.** Meanwhile, pulse the bread sticks in a food processor to crumbs, or crush them on a flat surface with a rolling pin. Spread on a plate.

**3.** Season the beef with salt and pepper, and dredge in the crumbs. Arrange on a platter.

**4.** Heat the salsa con queso in the microwave or a small saucepan, and transfer to a small serving bowl. Put the hot dog onions and chow-chow relish in separate small serving bowls.

**5.** Using skewers or fondue forks, invite your guests to skewer the beef and dip into the hot oil for about 45 seconds for rare. Serve with the dipping sauces.

# PIGS IN A BLANKET SWISS FONDUE

**Number of Servings: 4**  *Estimated Cost: $11*

*5 cups canola oil*
**2 packages frozen (about 30) pigs in a blanket**
**⅓ cup spicy brown mustard**
**¼ cup ketchup**

**1.** In a 4-quart fondue pot or saucepan, heat the oil to 400 degrees.

**2.** Holding each hot dog firmly in one hand, insert a skewer through the center length-wise. Arrange on a platter.

**3.** In a small bowl, mix together the mustard and ketchup to make a dipping sauce.

**4.** Invite your guests to cook the hot dogs in the hot oil for 1 minute, or until the pastry is golden brown, crisp, and puffy. Serve with the dipping sauce.

# Soups

# CHILLED CUCUMBER SOUP WITH SMOKED SALMON AND CRÈME FRAÎCHE

**Number of Servings: 4**  *Estimated Cost: $12*

2½ large cucumbers, 1 unpeeled, the other 1½ peeled,
cut into large chunks and chilled
1 large shallot, finely chopped
6 tablespoons chopped fresh dill, plus 4 small sprigs
*½ cup plus 1 tablespoon water*
*Salt and freshly ground black pepper*
½ cup crème fraîche
4 ounces thinly sliced smoked salmon

**1.** Combine the cucumbers, half of the shallot, and 3 tablespoons of the chopped dill in the bowl of a food processor and process until relatively smooth, with some very small chunks of cucumber. Add the ½ cup water and process to blend. Season well with salt and pepper. The soup can be chilled until ready to serve, if desired.

**2.** In a small bowl, combine the remaining shallot, 1 tablespoon water, and 3 tablespoons chopped dill with the crème fraîche. Season with salt and pepper.

**3.** Ladle the soup into 4 bowls and top each with a generous swirl of the crème fraîche. Arrange a few slices of smoked salmon in the center of each bowl. Garnish each bowl with a dill sprig, and serve.

# RICH MUSHROOM BOUILLON

**Number of Servings: 4**  *Estimated cost: $20*

*8 tablespoons (1 stick) butter, cut into 4 pieces*
**6 cups (1 pound) sliced wild mushrooms**
**⅓ cup finely chopped shallots**
**2 teaspoons chopped fresh thyme**
*Salt and freshly ground black pepper*
**⅔ cup dry sherry**
*2½ cups water*
**¼ cup chopped fresh chives**

**1.** Heat a very large straight-sided sauté pan until very hot. Add the butter and follow immediately with the mushrooms. Sauté until the mushrooms are lightly browned. Add the shallots and thyme and sauté until fragrant. Season generously with salt and pepper.

**2.** Add the sherry and the water and bring to a boil. Turn off the heat. Let the broth steep for approximately 2 minutes, taste, and adjust the seasoning. Add the chives and serve.

# MUSHROOM SOUP WITH BOURSIN CROUTONS

**Number of Servings: 4**  *Estimated Cost: $13.50*

**3 cups prepared creamy mushroom soup**
*Salt and freshly ground black pepper*
*2 tablespoons extra virgin olive oil, plus extra for drizzling*
**4 (½-inch-thick) diagonal slices baguette**
**1 (5.2-ounce) package Boursin cheese**
**¼ cup chopped fresh chives**
**4 large shiitake mushrooms, stems removed, thinly sliced**

**1.** Heat a large sauté pan over medium heat.

**2.** In a medium saucepan, heat the soup until simmering. Season with salt and pepper, if necessary.

**3.** Pour the olive oil into the hot pan and heat until hot but not smoking. Place the bread slices in the pan. Cook for about 1½ minutes on each side, or until golden brown and crisp. Remove from the pan and season with salt and pepper. Spread each toast with one-quarter of the cheese.

**4.** Add 3 tablespoons of the chives to the soup and stir. Ladle soup into four soup bowls. Scatter the raw shiitakes and the remaining 1 tablespoon chives over the soup, drizzle with olive oil, and lay a toast on the rim of each bowl. Serve.

# STRACCIATELLA

**Number of Servings: 4** *Estimated Cost: $6.50*

**4½ cups chicken broth**
**3 cups shredded escarole**
**3 eggs, beaten**
*Salt and freshly ground black pepper*
**⅔ cup grated Parmigiano-Reggiano cheese**

**1.** Bring the chicken broth to a simmer in a large pot. Add the escarole and return to a simmer. Simmer for 1 minute, then stir, add the eggs, and stir until they are just cooked, about 30 seconds. Turn off the heat. Season with salt and pepper.

**2.** To serve, divide the soup among four bowls. Sprinkle the Parmigiano-Reggiano cheese over the top.

# CORN AND CRAB CHOWDER WITH TARRAGON

**Number of Servings: 4**  *Estimated Cost: $17*

**2 (16-ounce) cans cream of corn soup**
*Salt and freshly ground black pepper*
**6 ounces fresh lump crabmeat, picked over for shells and cartilage**
**2 tablespoons chopped fresh tarragon**
*1 tablespoon extra virgin olive oil, plus extra, if desired, for drizzling*
**3 tablespoons chopped fresh chives**

**1.** Bring the soup to a simmer in a medium pot. Season with salt and pepper if necessary.

**2.** Meanwhile, in a small bowl, combine the crabmeat, tarragon, and olive oil. Season with salt and pepper.

**3.** Divide the crabmeat among four soup bowls and ladle the hot soup over the crabmeat. Sprinkle the chives on top and drizzle with olive oil, if desired. Serve immediately.

# HOT-AND-SOUR SHRIMP RICE NOODLE SOUP

**Number of Servings: 4**  *Estimated Cost: $6.25*

*6 cups water*

**2 teaspoons Thai hot curry paste, or to taste**

*1 tablespoon sugar*

**4 ounces rice noodles**

**6 tablespoons fish sauce**

*3 tablespoons white vinegar, or to taste*

**⅔ pound shrimp (30 to 40 count), peeled and deveined**

**¾ cup fresh cilantro leaves**

**1.** In a large saucepan, combine the water, curry paste, and sugar and bring to a boil over high heat. Add the rice noodles and cook for 1 minute, or until tender. Reduce the heat to a simmer and add the fish sauce, vinegar, and shrimp. Simmer until the shrimp are just cooked. Taste and adjust the seasoning to your liking: add more curry paste if you like it hotter; add more vinegar if you like a more sour flavor.

**2.** Stir the cilantro into the soup and divide among four bowls. Serve hot.

# TURKEY, GREEN ONION, AND RICE NOODLE SOUP

**Number of Servings: 4**  *Estimated Cost: $11*

*6 cups water*
**4 (1.6-ounce) packages Thai Kitchen Lemongrass and Chile Soup Mix**
**1 pound turkey cutlets, sliced into thin strips**
**2 tablespoons Maggi seasoning**
**1 bunch scallions, thinly sliced on the diagonal**
**1 cup fresh bean sprouts, rinsed**
*Salt and freshly ground black pepper*

**1.** Bring the water to a boil in a medium pot. Add the oil packet and seasoning packet from the soup mix. Add the turkey and turn the heat to the lowest setting; the broth should not even simmer. After 1 minute, add the rice noodles from the soup packet and let soften, about 3 minutes.

**2.** Bring the soup to a low simmer. Add the Maggi seasoning, scallions, and bean sprouts and stir to combine. Season with salt and pepper if necessary, and serve.

# BEEF SHABU-SHABU WITH WATERCRESS

**Number of Servings: 4**  *Estimated Cost: $17.75*

**6 cups chicken broth**
**¼ cup Dijon mustard**
**1 cup store-bought precooked scallop-cut potatoes**
*Salt and freshly ground black pepper*
**1 pound very thinly sliced deli roast beef**
**2 bunches watercress, trimmed and washed**

**1.** In a medium pot, bring the chicken broth to a boil. Whisk in the mustard.

**2.** Add the potatoes and simmer until they are hot and tender. Season with salt and pepper.

**3.** Arrange the roast beef slices in four bowls. Pour the broth and potatoes over the beef and scatter the watercress over the top. Serve immediately.

# ROAST BEEF BORSCHT

**Number of Servings: 4**  *Estimated Cost: $14.25*

**1 (16-ounce) jar borscht**
**1 (8-ounce) jar horseradish with beets**
**2 bunches scallions, cut diagonally into ½-inch slices**
**1 pound sliced deli roast beef, cut into ½-inch strips**
*Salt and freshly ground black pepper*
**¾ cup sour cream**

**1.** In a large pot, combine the borscht and horseradish and bring to a boil over high heat. Add the scallions and roast beef and stir to combine. Season with salt and pepper.

**2.** Ladle the soup into bowls and top each portion with 3 tablespoons sour cream. Serve.

# VIETNAMESE BEEF AND BASIL SOUP

**Number of Servings: 4**  *Estimated Cost: $12*

**3 (14-ounce) cans beef broth**
**3½ ounces rice noodles**
**½ cup chopped fresh basil**
**½ pound thinly sliced deli roast beef**
*4 teaspoons chili oil*
**2 limes, cut into wedges**

**1.** Bring the beef broth to a simmer in a large pot. Turn the heat to the lowest setting and add the rice noodles. Stir to separate the noodles, and allow to soften in the broth until tender, about 2 minutes.

**2.** Bring the soup back to a simmer. Turn off the heat and stir in the basil.

**3.** Divide the roast beef among four soup bowls. Ladle the soup into the bowls, distributing the noodles evenly. Drizzle 1 teaspoon chili oil over each bowl, and serve with the lime wedges.

# Salads

# AVOCADO SALAD WITH RED ONION AND FETA

**Number of Servings: 4**  *Estimated Cost: $15.25*

**Grated zest of 4 lemons, plus ½ cup fresh lemon juice**
*6 tablespoons extra virgin olive oil*
*Salt and freshly ground black pepper*
**1 large red onion, cut into very thin slices (about 1½ cups)**
**4 ripe avocados, pitted, peeled, and sliced**
**8 ounces feta cheese, crumbled**
**⅓ cup chopped fresh cilantro**

**1.** To make the dressing, combine the lemon zest, lemon juice, and olive oil in a bowl; season with salt and pepper. In another bowl, toss the red onions with half the dressing.

**2.** Lay out the slices of 1 avocado on each of four plates. Season with salt and pepper. Top with red onion and scatter the feta over the onions. Drizzle the remaining dressing evenly over the salads and sprinkle with the cilantro. Serve.

# PICO DE GALLO SALAD WITH AVOCADO

**Number of Servings: 4**  *Estimated Cost: $14.75*

¼ **cup fresh lime juice**
*¼ cup olive oil*
**2 large heads Boston lettuce, shredded**
⅔ **cup chopped fresh cilantro**
**1 (10-ounce) container pico de gallo or other fresh salsa**
*Salt and freshly ground black pepper*
**2 large ripe avocados**

**1.** In a small bowl, whisk together the lime juice and olive oil.

**2.** In a large bowl, combine the lettuce, cilantro, and pico de gallo. Season with salt and pepper, and toss with the lime juice dressing.

**3.** Cut the avocados in half and remove the pits. Squeeze each avocado half (as you would a lemon) so that the flesh comes out of the skin in chunks. Season with salt.

**4.** Add the avocado chunks to the salad and gently toss. Serve immediately.

# GOAT CHEESE, RADISH, AND DRIED CRANBERRY SALAD

**Number of Servings: 4**  *Estimated Cost: $15.50*

⅓ **cup salted peanuts**
½ **cup dried cranberries**
**3 cups radishes cut into 6 wedges each (about a 1-pound bag)**
½ **cup celery leaves**
**8 ounces fresh goat cheese, crumbled**
*½ cup extra virgin olive oil*
*Salt and freshly ground black pepper*

In a large bowl, toss the peanuts, dried cranberries, radishes, celery leaves, and goat cheese with the olive oil; be careful not to mash the goat cheese into the salad. Season with salt and pepper, and serve.

# PEAR AND STILTON SALAD

**Number of Servings: 4**  *Estimated Cost: $19.75*

**1 cup pecan halves**
*2 tablespoons sherry vinegar*
*¼ cup extra virgin olive oil*
**2 large heads frisée, trimmed and cut into bite-size pieces**
**3 tablespoons chopped fresh chives**
**3 ripe Anjou pears, cored and thinly sliced**
**8 ounces Stilton cheese, crumbled or cut into small cubes**
*Salt and freshly ground black pepper*

**1.** Preheat the oven to 400 degrees.

**2.** Spread the pecan halves on a baking sheet and toast in the oven for 5 minutes, or until they turn darker brown and very aromatic. Allow to cool. Lightly crush the pecans, if desired.

**3.** Whisk together the vinegar and olive oil in a small bowl.

**4.** In a large bowl, combine the frisée, chives, pears, cheese, and toasted pecans. Toss with the vinaigrette. Season with salt and pepper, and serve.

# TOMATO AND MOZZARELLA SALAD

**Number of Servings: 4** *Estimated Cost: $16.75*

**3 to 4 large ripe tomatoes**
*Salt and freshly ground black pepper*
**2 small shallots, chopped**
*¼ cup red wine vinegar*
**32 large fresh basil leaves**
**1½ pounds fresh mozzarella, cut into 16 slices**
*Extra virgin olive oil for drizzling*

**1.** Slice the tomatoes into 16 even slices and lay them out on a work surface. Season liberally with salt and pepper.

**2.** Mix the shallots with the vinegar in a small bowl.

**3.** To assemble each salad, lay 1 tomato slice at the far left side of a large plate. Top it with a basil leaf. Slightly overlap the tomato with a slice of mozzarella and top it with another basil leaf. Repeat this process three times so that you have a line of tomatoes, basil, and mozzarella running from the left side of the plate to the right side. Season the salads with more salt and freshly ground pepper, if desired.

**4.** Spoon the shallot mixture evenly over the salads and drizzle liberally with extra virgin olive oil. Serve.

# CHARRED MACKEREL WITH PEARS AND CAESAR DRESSING

**Number of Servings: 4**  *Estimated Cost: $16.75*

1¼ **pounds mackerel fillet, cut into 4 portions**
*2 tablespoons corn oil*
*Salt and freshly ground black pepper*
**2 ripe Anjou pears, cored and sliced**
**1 (10-ounce) bag romaine mix**
**1 (8-ounce) bottle creamy Caesar dressing**
**1 lemon, halved**

**1.** Heat a large skillet, preferably cast iron, until smoking.

**2.** Rub the skin side of the mackerel with the corn oil and season with salt and pepper. Place the mackerel skin side down in the pan and press down firmly on each fillet with a spatula. Cook for about 5 minutes, or until the skin is charred and fish is cooked to desired doneness. Turn the mackerel over, then immediately remove from the pan and transfer to a plate.

**3.** In a large bowl, toss the pears and romaine with the dressing. Divide the salad among four plates. Place a mackerel fillet on top of each romaine-pear bed. Squeeze fresh lemon juice over each salad, and serve.

# SHRIMP SALAD WITH RED ONION, MANGO, AND CILANTRO

**Number of Servings: 4** *Estimated Cost: $20*

1½ **pounds shrimp (36 to 40 count), peeled and deveined**
*Salt and freshly ground black pepper*
*2 tablespoons chili oil*
**2 mangoes, peeled, pitted, and diced**
**1 large red onion, finely diced**
**1 cup chopped fresh cilantro**
½ **cup fresh lime juice**

**1.** Heat a large sauté pan until smoking.

**2.** Season the shrimp with salt and pepper. Add the chili oil to the hot pan, then add the shrimp to the pan and cook for about 2 minutes per side. Remove from the heat.

**3.** In a large bowl, combine the shrimp with the mangoes, onion, cilantro, and lime juice. Toss and season with salt and pepper to taste. Serve immediately, or chill, if desired, and serve cold.

# CHICKEN, GOAT CHEESE, AND BLOOD ORANGE SALAD

**Number of Servings: 4**  *Estimated Cost: $20*

⅓ **cup sunflower seeds**

**4 blood or navel oranges, peel and pith removed and cut into ⅓-inch slices, 1 tablespoon juice reserved**

*2 tablespoons sherry vinegar*

*¼ cup extra virgin olive oil*

**1 rotisserie chicken (about 2 pounds), skin removed and meat cut into large pieces**

**8 ounces goat cheese, crumbled**

**7 ounces mesclun salad greens**

*Salt and freshly ground black pepper*

**1.** Preheat the oven to 425 degrees.

**2.** Spread the sunflower seeds on a baking sheet and toast in the oven for 5 minutes, or until lightly browned and aromatic. Set aside to cool.

**3.** Meanwhile, combine the 1 tablespoon orange juice with the sherry vinegar in a small bowl. Whisk in the olive oil.

**4.** In a large bowl, combine the oranges, chicken, goat cheese, and mesclun. Season with salt and pepper and toss gently with the dressing, being careful not to mash the goat cheese.

**5.** Divide the salad among four large plates, scatter the toasted seeds, and serve.

# BUFFALO CHICKEN TENDERS WITH CELERY AND BLUE CHEESE SALAD

**Number of Servings: 4**  *Estimated Cost: $20*

*3 quarts canola oil*
**1½ pounds chicken tenders**
*Corn flour or masa harina for dredging*
*Salt and freshly ground black pepper*
**¾ cup bottled buffalo wing sauce**
**2 celery hearts, sliced diagonally**
**1¼ cups crumbled blue cheese**
**⅔ cup mayonnaise**

**1.** In a large pot, heat the oil to 400 degrees.

**2.** Dredge the chicken tenders in corn flour. Add to the hot oil and cook for about 5 minutes, stirring occasionally, or until golden brown and cooked through. Drain on paper towels and season with salt and pepper. In a large bowl, toss the tenders with the buffalo wing sauce.

**3.** Meanwhile, combine the celery, blue cheese, and mayonnaise in a large bowl. Stir to coat the celery, and season with salt and pepper. Set aside.

**4.** To serve, divide the celery salad among four plates and pile an equal amount of chicken tenders on top of each salad.

# PEANUT CHICKEN AND RADICCHIO SALAD

**Number of Servings: 4**  *Estimated Cost: $14.25*

2½ pounds roasted chicken breast, shredded
1¼ cups Thai peanut sauce
3 oranges, peeled and segmented
*Salt and freshly ground black pepper*
1 (¾-pound) head radicchio, sliced crosswise into ½-inch-wide strips
½ cup salted peanuts

**1.** In a medium bowl, thoroughly combine the chicken and peanut sauce. Gently stir in the orange segments. Season with salt and pepper.

**2.** Form a bed of radicchio on each of four plates. Pile the chicken salad on top. Drizzle with any dressing remaining in the bowl. Sprinkle the peanuts over the salads, and serve.

# CHICKEN AND CHOPPED SALAD

**Number of Servings: 4**  *Estimated Cost: $11.50*

*½ cup vegetable oil*
**4 thin-cut chicken breast cutlets**
*Salt and freshly ground black pepper*
*½ cup flour*
**2 eggs**
**6 cups sliced iceberg lettuce**
**6 tablespoons India relish**
**⅔ cup Dijonnaise**

**1.** Heat the oil in a large nonstick sauté pan until very hot.

**2.** Meanwhile, season the chicken with salt and pepper and dredge in the flour. Beat the eggs in a shallow bowl.

**3.** When the oil is hot, dip the chicken into the eggs to coat and place in the pan. Cook until golden on the first side. Turn and cook until the other side is golden, about 3 to 4 minutes total. Drain on paper towels.

**4.** Meanwhile, in a large bowl, toss the lettuce with the relish and Dijonnaise. Season with salt and pepper to taste.

**5.** Divide the salad among four plates. Place a chicken breast on top of each salad. Serve immediately.

# WARM WALDORF CHICKEN SALAD

**Number of Servings: 4**  *Estimated Cost: $14.25*

⅔ **cup raisins**
*3 tablespoons sherry vinegar*
*2 tablespoons canola oil*
**2 Granny Smith apples, cored and sliced**
**1 cup celery hearts, sliced on the diagonal**
*Salt and freshly ground black pepper*
**2 rotisserie chickens (about 2 pounds each),
skin removed and meat shredded**
**1 cup mayonnaise**

**1.** Place the raisins and sherry vinegar in a small bowl and microwave for about 2 minutes, or until the raisins have plumped in the vinegar. Or, steep the raisins overnight in the vinegar. Set aside.

**2.** Heat the oil in a large sauté pan until smoking. Add the apples and celery, season with salt and pepper, and sauté, stirring frequently, for about 2 minutes, or until the apples and celery are hot but still crunchy.

**3.** Turn off the heat and add the raisins, chicken, and mayonnaise to the pan. Toss well to combine. Season with salt and pepper. Serve immediately.

# CHILLED PORK TENDERLOIN SALAD WITH CHOPPED OLIVE DRESSING

**Number of Servings: 4**  *Estimated Cost: $20*

**1 cup pitted mixed olives**
**2 (5-ounce) jars marinated artichoke hearts, drained,**
**6 tablespoons liquid reserved**
*¼ cup extra virgin olive oil*
**8 ounces ricotta salata cheese, crumbled or cut into small cubes**
**1 pound leftover cooked pork tenderloin, thinly sliced**
**7 ounces baby arugula**
*Salt and freshly ground black pepper*

**1.** Roughly chop the olives. Combine with 4 tablespoons of the reserved artichoke liquid and the olive oil in a small bowl.

**2.** In a large bowl, toss together the artichoke hearts, ricotta salata, and pork with half the olive dressing.

**3.** In another large bowl, toss the arugula with the remaining 2 tablespoons artichoke liquid. Season with salt and pepper.

**4.** Divide the arugula among four plates. Arrange the pork salad on top of the arugula equally among the plates. Drizzle the remaining dressing over the salads. Serve.

# PROSCIUTTO, PARMIGIANO, PIMIENTO, AND ARUGULA SALAD

**Number of Servings: 4** *Estimated Cost: $19.50*

**2 tablespoons Dijon mustard**
*2 tablespoons white vinegar*
*6 tablespoons extra virgin olive oil*
**8 cups baby arugula**
**1½ cups sliced pimientos, drained**
*Salt and freshly ground black pepper*
**7 ounces thinly sliced prosciutto**
**An 8-ounce wedge Parmigiano-Reggiano cheese**

**1.** Whisk together the mustard and vinegar in a small bowl. To make the vinaigrette, whisk in olive oil.

**2.** In a large bowl, combine the arugula and pimientos. Toss gently with the vinaigrette. Season with salt and pepper, and gently fold in the prosciutto.

**3.** Arrange the salad on four plates. With a vegetable peeler, shave curls off the chunk of Parmigiano-Reggiano cheese over each salad. Serve.

# Sandwiches

# HOT CHICKEN AND BRIE SANDWICH WITH TOASTED PECANS

**Number of Servings: 4**  *Estimated Cost: $17.50*

*7 tablespoons butter*
**4 large slices Italian sourdough bread (cut ¾ inch thick)**
*Salt*
**1 pound Brie cheese, cut into thin slices**
**1 rotisserie chicken (about 2 pounds), skin removed and meat torn into chunks**
*Freshly ground black pepper*
**1¼ cups pecan halves**

**1.** Preheat a toaster oven to high or turn on the oven broiler and heat a large sauté pan until smoking.

**2.** Spread 1 tablespoon butter on both sides of each piece of bread; season with salt. Place in the toaster oven or under the broiler and toast for about a minute, or until golden brown and crunchy on the outside.

**3.** Remove the bread from the oven and lay half of the Brie on top of the bread. Divide the chicken into 4 portions and pile on top of the Brie. Top the chicken with the remaining Brie. Season the sandwiches with salt and pepper and return to the toaster oven or broiler. Toast until the cheese is melted completely, about 4 more minutes.

**4.** Meanwhile, melt the remaining 3 tablespoons butter in the hot pan. Add the pecan halves and cook, stirring and tossing often, until they turn darker brown and develop a rich toasted aroma. Season with salt and pepper, and drain on paper towels.

**5.** Top each sandwich with one-quarter of the pecans, and serve.

# HOT TURKEY "COLESLAW" SANDWICH

**Number of Servings: 4** *Estimated Cost: $13*

**1 pound thinly sliced roasted turkey breast**
**4 slices cinnamon raisin swirl bread**
*Salt and freshly ground black pepper*
**3½ cups prepared sweet-and-sour red cabbage, drained**
**¼ cup jalapeño vinegar (or liquid from pickled jalapeños)**
**3 tablespoons honey**

**1.** Preheat a toaster oven to high or turn on the oven broiler.

**2.** Divide the turkey into 4 portions and pile evenly on the bread. Season with salt and pepper.

**3.** Toss the cabbage, jalapeño vinegar, and honey together and season with salt and pepper. Spread this "coleslaw" evenly over the turkey.

**4.** Place the sandwiches in the toaster oven or under the broiler and toast for 5 minutes, watching to make sure they don't burn. Serve.

# MUSHROOM AND RED ONION BURGERS

**Number of Servings: 4**  *Estimated Cost: $12*

**2 cups chopped mushrooms of your choice**
**¼ cup pickled jalapeños, chopped**
**1 pound ground beef**
*Salt and freshly ground black pepper*
**½ red onion, thinly sliced**
**4 hamburger buns, split**

**1.** Preheat a grill pan until very hot.

**2.** In a medium bowl, mix the mushrooms, jalapeños, and ground beef and season thoroughly with salt and pepper. Divide the mixture into 4 equal portions, and form each into a ¾- to 1-inch-thick patty. Season again with salt and pepper if necessary.

**3.** Place the patties on the grill. Cook for about 2½ minutes, and turn. Top each burger with a few slices of onion, and cook for another 2½ minutes, or until the desired doneness.

**4.** Place the burgers on the buns, and serve with your favorite condiments.

# ROAST BEEF WRAP WITH GARLIC RELISH

**Number of Servings: 4**  *Estimated Cost: $18.50*

**4 large flatbreads, lavash, or large flour tortillas**
**1 cup plain yogurt, preferably Greek**
**¼ cup prepared garlic relish**
**1 pound thinly sliced roast beef**
**3 cups baby arugula**
*Salt and freshly ground black pepper*

**1.** Preheat a grill pan until very hot.

**2.** Place the flatbreads on the grill and cook them, turning once, until they are hot and have grill marks on both sides, about 45 seconds per side.

**3.** Meanwhile, in a medium bowl, combine the yogurt and garlic relish.

**4.** To assemble the wraps, lay the flatbreads on a work surface. Spread some of the yogurt mixture on each and then top each with a thin layer of roast beef. Continue with alternating layers of the remaining yogurt and roast beef, finishing with yogurt. Scatter the arugula on top and season well with salt and pepper. Roll each flatbread up tightly and secure with a toothpick or small skewer. Serve.

# HAM ON RYE WITH ARTICHOKES AND DIJON

**Number of Servings: 4**  *Estimated Cost: $15*

*4 tablespoons butter, softened*
**6 tablespoons Dijon mustard**
**1 (14-ounce) can artichoke hearts, drained and chopped**
**½ Vidalia onion, very thinly sliced**
*Salt and freshly ground black pepper*
**1 pound sliced honey ham**
**4 slices rye bread**

**1.** Preheat a toaster oven to high or turn on the oven broiler.

**2.** In a medium bowl, beat together the butter and mustard until well blended. Add the artichokes and onion and season with salt and pepper. Toss until evenly coated. Set aside.

**3.** Divide the ham equally among the slices of bread. Top with the artichoke mixture and spread evenly over the ham.

**4.** Place the sandwiches in the toaster oven or under the broiler and toast for 5 minutes, or until the tops are golden brown. Serve.

# TOASTED HOT DOG REUBEN

**Number of Servings: 4**  *Estimated Cost: $17.75*

**6 hot dogs**
**8 slices rye bread**
**8 (1-ounce) slices Swiss cheese**
**1½ cups sauerkraut, drained well**
**½ cup Thousand Island dressing**

**1.** Preheat a panini press or turn on the broiler.

**2.** Slice each hot dog crosswise in half, then cut lengthwise into ½-inch-thick slices.

**3.** Lay 4 slices of bread on a work surface. Cover each piece of bread with a slice of cheese and one-quarter of the hot dog slices. Pile the sauerkraut on top of the hot dog slices. Spoon 2 tablespoons of the dressing evenly over each mound of sauerkraut and top with the remaining cheese, then the remaining bread. Place in the panini press, or under the broiler, and cook until the cheese is melted and sandwich is hot throughout, about 5 minutes. Serve hot.

# Panini

# FETA AND KALAMATA PANINI

**Number of Servings: 4** *Estimated Cost: $17.50*

**4 Portuguese or sandwich rolls, split**
**12 ounces feta cheese, cut into thin slices**
**1 cup jarred roasted red peppers, cut into thin strips**
**½ cup chopped Kalamata olives**
**2 small fennel bulbs, shaved or thinly sliced, green tops reserved**
*1½ tablespoons sherry vinegar*
*2 tablespoons extra virgin olive oil*
*Salt and freshly ground black pepper*

**1.** Preheat a panini press on the highest setting. Or heat a large nonstick frying pan over medium heat for several minutes.

**2.** Lay out the bottoms of the rolls on a work surface. Cover with half of the cheese slices. Top the cheese with the red peppers and the olives. Top with the remaining cheese and then with the top halves of the rolls.

**3.** Place the sandwiches in the panini press or in the frying pan. If using a frying pan, weight the sandwiches by placing a cake pan (smaller than the diameter of your frying pan) over them and placing a heavy can of similar weight in the cake pan; turn the sandwiches with a spatula midway through the cooking time, replacing the cake pan and weight. Cook for 5 minutes, or until the bread is crisp and the cheese is melted.

**4.** Meanwhile, toss the fennel with the sherry vinegar and the olive oil in a bowl. Chop the reserved fennel greens and add to the salad. Season with salt and pepper.

**5.** When the sandwiches are ready, slice in half and serve each with a mound of the fennel salad.

# SMOKED SALMON AND SWISS CHEESE PANINI

**Number of Servings: 4** *Estimated Cost: $18*

½ cup piccalilli relish
8 slices pumpernickel bread
8 ounces sliced Swiss cheese
10 to 12 ounces thinly sliced smoked salmon
2 celery hearts, each trimmed to 4 inches and quartered

**1.** Preheat a panini press. Or heat a large nonstick frying pan over medium heat for several minutes.

**2.** Spread 1 tablespoon of the piccalilli evenly on each slice of bread. Layer the Swiss cheese and salmon on 4 of the slices, and top with the remaining 4 slices of bread.

**3.** Place the sandwiches in the panini press or frying pan. If using a frying pan, weight the sandwiches by placing a cake pan (smaller than the diameter of your frying pan) over them and placing a heavy can of similar weight in the cake pan; turn the sandwiches with a spatula midway through the cooking time, replacing the cake pan and weight. Cook for 4 minutes, or until the bread is crispy and the cheese is melted; be careful not to let the salmon cook. Remove the sandwiches from the press or pan, slice in half, and serve with the celery.

# ROAST BEEF AND BOURSIN PANINI

**Number of Servings: 4** *Estimated Cost: $20*

**4 slices crusty Italian or semolina bread**
**1½ (5.2-ounce) packages Boursin cheese, softened**
**¼ cup chopped cocktail onions**
**1 pound sliced deli roast beef**
*Salt and freshly ground black pepper*
**2 cups radishes, washed and quartered**

**1.** Preheat a panini press. Or heat a large nonstick frying pan over medium heat for several minutes.

**2.** Slice each piece of bread lengthwise in half. Spread each slice with Boursin cheese. Scatter the pickled onions over the 4 bottom halves of the bread slices. Top with the roast beef and season with salt and pepper. Cover with the remaining bread.

**3.** Place the sandwiches in the panini press or frying pan. If using a frying pan, weight the sandwiches by placing a cake pan (smaller than the diameter of your frying pan) over them and placing a heavy can of similar weight in the cake pan; turn the sandwiches with a spatula midway through the cooking time, replacing the cake pan and weight. Cook for 5 minutes, or until the cheese is melted and the bread is crisp. Cut the sandwiches in half and serve with the radishes.

# PROSCIUTTO, MOZZARELLA, AND TOMATO PANINI

**Number of Servings: 4** *Estimated Cost: $14.50*

**4 large slices crusty Italian bread, split in half**
**12 ounces fresh mozzarella, thinly sliced**
**6 ounces thinly sliced prosciutto**
**2 ripe tomatoes, thinly sliced**
**½ cup fresh basil leaves**
*Salt and freshly ground black pepper*
*¼ cup extra virgin olive oil*

**1.** Preheat a panini press. Or heat a large nonstick frying pan over medium heat for several minutes.

**2.** Lay the bread on a work surface and layer the mozzarella, prosciutto, tomatoes, and basil on each slice. Season well with salt and pepper and drizzle with the olive oil. Close the sandwiches.

**3.** Place the sandwiches in the panini press or frying pan. If using a frying pan, weight the sandwiches by placing a cake pan (smaller than the diameter of your frying pan) over them and placing a heavy can of similar weight in the cake pan; turn the sandwiches with a spatula midway through the cooking time, replacing the cake pan and weight. Cook until the cheese is melted, about 5 minutes total. Cut in half and serve.

# HAM AND GORGONZOLA PANINI

**Number of Servings: 4**  *Estimated Cost: $19*

6 ounces Gorgonzola cheese, thinly sliced
4 Portuguese or sandwich rolls, split
1 pound thinly sliced honey ham
½ cup prepared sweet Vidalia onion condiment
2 large fennel bulbs, trimmed and each cut into 8 wedges

**1.** Preheat a panini press. Or heat a large nonstick frying pan over medium heat for several minutes.

**2.** Lay half of the cheese on the bottom halves of the rolls. Layer on the ham and onions, then top with the remaining cheese. Cover each sandwich with the top half of the roll.

**3.** Place the sandwiches in the panini press or frying pan. If using a frying pan, weight the sandwiches by placing a cake pan (smaller than the diameter of your frying pan) over them and placing a heavy can of similar weight in the cake pan; turn the sandwiches with a spatula midway through the cooking time, replacing the cake pan and weight. Cook until the cheese is melted and the bread is crispy, about 5 minutes total. Slice the sandwiches in half, and serve with the fennel.

# Sides

# ALL-PURPOSE MUSHROOM MIX

**Yield: About 2½ cups**  *Estimated Cost: $7 with cultivated mushrooms, $18 with a mix of wild mushrooms*

*8 tablespoons (1 stick) unsalted butter*
**6 cups sliced wild or cultivated mushrooms**
**¼ cup finely chopped shallots**
**2 teaspoons chopped fresh thyme**
**⅓ cup sweet white wine**
*Salt and freshly ground black pepper*

**1.** Heat a large sauté pan until smoking. Add the butter to the pan and follow immediately with the mushrooms. Sauté for about 1 minute, stirring as the mushrooms begin to take on color.

**2.** Push aside the mushrooms to clear a small space on one side of the pan. Add the shallots and cook, stirring occasionally, until fragrant. Mix the shallots and the thyme into the mushrooms.

**3.** Add the wine and simmer until evaporated. Season with salt and pepper to taste. Serve.

# CANNELLINI WITH TRICOLOR PEPPERS, TOMATO, AND PARSLEY

**Number of Servings: 4** *Estimated Cost: $6.75*

*2 tablespoons olive oil*
**1 (7-ounce) package diced red, green, and yellow bell peppers**
*Salt and freshly ground black pepper*
**2 cloves garlic, chopped**
**⅓ cup tomato paste**
**2 (15-ounce) cans cannellini, 1 can drained**
**⅓ cup chopped flat-leaf parsley**

**1.** Heat the oil in a large sauté pan. Add the peppers, season with salt and pepper, and sauté, stirring frequently, until almost tender. Push the peppers aside to clear a small space on one side of the pan and add the garlic. Cook, stirring, until the garlic is fragrant. Then mix the garlic into the peppers.

**2.** Add the tomato paste and beans to the pan, mixing thoroughly. Cook until the beans are heated through, adding a little water if necessary. Season with salt and pepper, and sprinkle the parsley over all. Serve.

# GOOD OL' RICE AND BEANS

**Number of Servings: 4**  *Estimated Cost: $4*

*2¼ cups water*
**1½ teaspoons ground achiote**
*1¼ teaspoons salt*
**2½ cups instant rice**
**1 (15-ounce) can black beans**
**½ cup chopped fresh cilantro**
**2 limes, cut into wedges**

**1.** In a medium saucepan, bring the water, achiote, and salt to a boil. Add the rice, stir, and cover. Turn off the heat and allow the rice to stand for 5 minutes.

**2.** Meanwhile, pour the beans into a medium bowl or a saucepan and heat in the microwave for 3 minutes, or heat on the stovetop until completely hot. Drain.

**3.** Stir the beans and cilantro into the rice. Season with additional salt if necessary. Serve with the lime wedges.

# MAMMA'S VEGETABLE GIAMBOTTA

**Number of Servings: 4**  *Estimated Cost: $14*

¼ *cup extra virgin olive oil*
**3 cups mixed wild mushrooms, sliced into bite-size pieces**
**1¼ cups (½-inch) cubanelle peppers, sliced**
**1 cup store-bought precooked cubed Bliss potatoes**
**1½ cups tomato puree**
*Salt and freshly ground black pepper*
**⅓ cup shredded fresh basil**

**1.** In a large sauté pan, heat the olive oil over medium-high heat.

**2.** Add the mushrooms and cubanelle peppers and cook for 2 minutes, stirring occasionally. Add the potatoes and cook for 1 minute. Stir in the tomato puree and cook until the mixture is heated through, about 2 minutes more. Season with salt and pepper, add the basil, and serve.

# SCALLOPED POTATOES WITH GRUYÈRE CHEESE AND MUSHROOMS

**Number of Servings: 4**  *Estimated Cost: $13*

**1½ pounds store-bought precooked scallop-cut potatoes**
**1½ cups thinly sliced shiitake mushrooms**
**7 ounces gruyère cheese, grated**
*Salt and freshly ground black pepper*
**½ cup heavy cream**

**1.** Preheat the broiler.

**2.** Spread the potatoes in a 13 x 17-inch baking dish. Scatter the mushrooms over the potatoes and sprinkle the cheese evenly over all. Season with salt and pepper and drizzle with the cream. Microwave on high for 4 minutes.

**3.** Place the dish under the broiler for 1 minute, or until the cheese is bubbling and beginning to turn golden brown. Serve.

# SOFT POLENTA WITH WILD MUSHROOMS

**Number of Servings: 4** *Estimated Cost: $15.75*

4 cups water
6 cloves garlic, chopped
1 (¾ ounce) package fresh thyme, leaves picked and chopped
*8 tablespoons (1 stick) butter*
4 cups mixed wild mushrooms, torn or cut into 1-inch pieces
*Salt and freshly ground black pepper*
¾ cup instant polenta
1¼ cups grated Pecorino-Romano cheese

**1.** Combine the water, two-thirds of the garlic, and half of the thyme in a medium saucepan. Bring to a simmer over high heat.

**2.** Meanwhile, heat a large sauté pan over high heat. When hot, add half the butter, then the mushrooms and remaining thyme. Sauté, stirring occasionally, for about 3 minutes.

**3.** Clear a small space on one side of the pan and add the remaining garlic. Cook, stirring, until the garlic is fragrant. Stir the garlic into the mushrooms. Season with salt and pepper. Keep warm over low heat.

**4.** Once the water simmers, gradually sprinkle in the polenta, whisking constantly, for about 3 minutes, or until the polenta absorbs all the liquid and is tender. Whisk in the cheese and remaining butter. Season with salt and pepper and pour into a large bowl.

**5.** Spoon the mushrooms over the polenta and serve.

# Vegetarian Main Dishes

# BASIL AND POTATO FRITTATA WITH FRISÉE

**Number of Servings: 4**  *Estimated Cost: $8*

*6 tablespoons olive oil*
**2 cups store-bought precooked cubed golden potatoes**
*Salt and freshly ground black pepper*
**12 eggs**
**⅓ cup chopped fresh basil**
*1 tablespoon plus 2 teaspoons sherry vinegar*
**7 ounces frisée, cut into bite-size pieces**
**An 8-ounce wedge Parmigiano-Reggiano cheese**

**1.** Preheat the oven to 500 degrees.

**2.** Heat ¼ cup of the olive oil in a large ovenproof sauté pan until smoking. Add the potatoes, season with salt and pepper, and cook for about 2 minutes.

**3.** Meanwhile, beat the eggs in a bowl. Season well with salt and pepper and mix in the basil. Add the eggs to the pan. Stir until the eggs begin to form large curds but are still wet.

**4.** Smooth the top of the mixture so that it is level. Place the pan in the oven and cook for about 2 minutes, or until set. Remove from the oven and loosen the sides of the frittata with a spatula. Invert onto a large plate or cutting board and slice into wedges.

**5.** Meanwhile, mix together the remaining 2 tablespoons olive oil and the sherry vinegar. Toss the frisée with this vinaigrette and season with salt and pepper. With a vegetable peeler, shave curls from the chunk of Parmigiano-Reggiano onto the salad. Serve the salad alongside the wedges of frittata.

# EGGPLANT PARMIGIANO

**Number of Servings: 4**  *Estimated Cost: $18.50*

*2 cups canola oil*
**2 cups prepared Fra Diavolo Sauce**
**2 large eggplants**
*Flour for dredging*
*Salt and freshly ground black pepper*
**3 eggs**
**3 cups dried bread crumbs**
**8 ounces sharp provolone cheese, thinly sliced**

**1.** Heat 1 cup of the oil in each of two large sauté pans. Heat the fra diavolo sauce in a microwave for about 3 minutes, or heat on the stovetop over medium-high heat until very hot; stir once during heating. Keep warm.

**2.** Meanwhile, trim each eggplant to about 5 inches long and 4 inches wide. Slice lengthwise into ⅜-inch-thick slices; you will need 8 slices total. Spread the flour on a plate and season with salt and pepper. Beat the eggs in a shallow dish. Spread the bread crumbs on another plate.

**3.** Lay 4 eggplant slices out on a work surface and cover each with one-quarter of the provolone. Top with the remaining 4 eggplant slices and press down firmly. Dredge the stacks in the flour, then in the eggs, then in the bread crumbs to coat. Season well with salt and pepper.

**4.** Place 2 eggplant stacks in each sauté pan and cook for 2½ minutes per side, or until they are golden brown and crispy and the cheese is melted. Place one stack on each plate, top with about ½ cup fra diavolo sauce, and serve.

# RED ONION FRITTATA WITH BABY SPINACH

**Number of Servings: 4**  *Estimated Cost: $9.25*

*3 tablespoons canola oil*
**3 medium-large red onions, very thinly sliced**
*Salt and freshly ground black pepper*
**12 eggs**
**7 ounces baby spinach**
*2 tablespoons sherry vinegar*
*¼ cup extra virgin olive oil*

**1.** Preheat the oven to 500 degrees.

**2.** Heat the canola oil in a large ovenproof sauté pan until hot. Add the onions, season with salt and pepper, and cook until tender, about 3 minutes.

**3.** Meanwhile, beat the eggs in a bowl. Season with salt and pepper, and add to the pan. Stir until they begin to form large curds but are still wet.

**4.** Place the frittata in the oven for about 2 minutes, or until the eggs have just set. Remove from the oven and loosen the sides of the frittata with a rubber spatula. Invert the frittata onto a large plate or a cutting board and cut into wedges.

**5.** In a large bowl, toss the spinach with the vinegar and olive oil. Season with salt and pepper. Serve a small mound of salad alongside each wedge of frittata.

# SOFT SCRAMBLED EGGS WITH ASPARAGUS ON TOASTED CROISSANTS

**Number of Servings: 4**  *Estimated Cost: $13.25*

**4 medium croissants, split**
*4 tablespoons butter*
**16 asparagus spears, tough ends trimmed and thinly sliced**
**3 large shallots, minced**
*Salt and freshly ground black pepper*
**12 eggs**
**2 tablespoons chopped fresh tarragon**

**1.** Preheat the toaster oven to high or turn on the oven broiler. Place the croissants cut side up in the toaster oven or under the broiler and toast until golden brown and crisp, about 1 minute.

**2.** Meanwhile, heat a large sauté pan. Add the butter. When it melts and bubbles, add the asparagus and shallots, season with salt and pepper, and cook until tender, about 3 minutes.

**3.** Beat the eggs in a bowl. Season with salt and pepper and add to the pan. Stir gently to scramble the eggs. When the eggs start to set, turn off the heat; the "carry-over" heat will finish cooking the eggs. Be careful not to overcook them.

**4.** To serve, place 2 croissant halves on each plate and spoon one-quarter of the scrambled egg mixture on top. Sprinkle with the tarragon and serve.

# TOFU AND RED PEPPER FLASH-FRY

**Number of Servings: 4**  *Estimated Cost: $13.50*

*2 quarts corn oil*
*Flour for dredging*
*Salt and freshly ground black pepper*
**4 eggs**
**1¼ pounds tofu, sliced 1 inch thick**
**2 red bell peppers, cored, seeded, and sliced**
**1¼ cups prepared garlic rib sauce**
**1 large bunch scallions, sliced thin**

**1.** Heat the oil in a large pot until very hot but not smoking, about 400 degrees.

**2.** Meanwhile, spread the flour on a plate and season with salt and pepper. Beat the eggs in a shallow dish. Dredge the tofu and peppers in the flour, then dip in the beaten eggs to coat. Add to the hot oil and stir gently to make sure the ingredients do not stick together. Cook for about 5 minutes, until golden and crisp. Drain on paper towels and season with salt and pepper.

**3.** Place the tofu and peppers in a large bowl and toss with the sauce and scallions. Serve immediately.

# WHITE BEAN AND MUSHROOM CHILI

**Number of Servings: 4**  *Estimated Cost: $11.25*

*⅓ cup extra virgin olive oil*
**1 small onion, diced**
**6 cups sliced portabella mushrooms**
*Salt and freshly ground black pepper*
**1 (15-ounce) can cannellini beans, drained**
**2 cups prepared marinara sauce**
**1 tablespoon chili powder**

**1.** In a large sauté pan, heat the olive oil until hot but not smoking. Add the onion and cook for 1 minute, or until it starts to soften. Add the portabellas and cook for another 2 minutes. Season well with salt and pepper.

**2.** Add the beans, marinara sauce, and chili powder and bring to a simmer. Taste to check the seasoning, and serve hot.

# Pasta and Noodle Main Dishes

# RICE NOODLES WITH SPICY PEANUT SAUCE

**Number of Servings: 4**  *Estimated Cost: $12*

**1 pound wide rice noodles**
*⅔ cup canola oil*
**1 (10-ounce) package sliced peppers and onions**
*Salt*
**1 (11.5-ounce) jar peanut sauce**
**½ cup chopped fresh cilantro**
**½ cup salted peanuts**

**1.** In a large bowl, cover the rice noodles with hot water and stir to separate the noodles. Allow to soak for 30 minutes; drain well.

**2.** Heat ¼ cup of the oil in each of two large sauté pans until hot but not smoking. Divide the peppers and onions between the two pans and stir-fry for about 2 minutes. Season with salt. Add half of the noodles to each pan and stir-fry for another 3 minutes, or until the noodles are cooked through.

**3.** Transfer the noodles to a large serving bowl, add the sauce and cilantro, and toss to coat. Season with salt if necessary, and sprinkle the peanuts on top. Serve hot.

# GNOCCHI WITH TOASTED GARLIC, WALNUTS, AND BITTER GREENS

**Number of Servings: 4**  *Estimated Cost: $18.50*

**2 (17.5-ounce) packages fresh potato gnocchi**
*¾ cup extra virgin olive oil*
**5 cloves garlic, chopped**
**1¼ cups walnut halves, slightly crushed**
**3 cups packaged mixed bitter greens (collard, mustard, and turnip greens)**
*Salt and freshly ground black pepper*
**1 cup grated Pecorino-Romano cheese**

**1.** Bring a large pot of salted water to a boil. Add the gnocchi and cook according to the package instructions. Drain.

**2.** Meanwhile, heat the olive oil in a large sauté pan until hot. Add the garlic and walnuts and cook until the garlic is a deep golden brown and nuts are aromatic, about 3 minutes. Add the greens and season with salt and pepper. Cook, stirring frequently, until the greens are wilted.

**3.** Add the gnocchi to the pan and toss to coat. Sprinkle with the Pecorino-Romano. Taste and adjust the seasoning if necessary. Serve immediately.

# CAPELLINI WITH LITTLENECK CLAMS

**Number of Servings: 4**  *Estimated Cost: $19.25*

*Salt*
**1 pound capellini (angel hair pasta)**
*⅔ cup extra virgin olive oil*
**4 large cloves garlic, chopped**
**1¼ teaspoons red pepper flakes**
**1 cup bottled clam juice**
**3 dozen littleneck clams, scrubbed**

**1.** Bring a large pot of salted water to a boil. Add the capellini and cook according to the package instructions. Drain.

**2.** Meanwhile, in a large pot, heat the olive oil until hot but not smoking. Add the garlic and red pepper flakes and cook until the garlic is a deep golden brown. Add the clam juice and bring to a rolling boil.

**3.** Add the clams to the pot, cover, and cook just until the clams open, about 2½ minutes.

**4.** Toss the capellini with the clam mixture. Taste, and adjust the seasoning if necessary. Serve hot.

# CAPELLINI ALLA PUTTANESCA

**Number of Servings: 4**  *Estimated Cost: $15*

*Salt*
**1 pound capellini (angel hair pasta)**
*¼ cup extra virgin olive oil*
**5 cloves garlic, thinly sliced**
**10 anchovy fillets, chopped**
**1 (24-ounce) jar fra diavolo sauce**
**3 tablespoons capers**

**1.** Bring a large pot of salted water to a boil. Add the pasta and cook according to the package instructions. Drain.

**2.** Meanwhile, heat the olive oil in a large sauté pan until hot. Add the garlic and sauté for 1 minute, stirring constantly. Add the anchovies and cook for 1 minute, mashing the anchovies with the back of a spoon. Add the sauce and capers and bring to a simmer.

**3.** Toss the pasta with the sauce. Serve hot.

# HANDKERCHIEF PASTA WITH LOBSTER, BOK CHOY, AND LEMON CREAM SAUCE

**Number of Servings: 4**  *Estimated Cost: $19.50*

**10 ounces fresh pasta sheets**
*2 tablespoons corn oil*
**1½ large heads bok choy, sliced crosswise (about 9 cups)**
*Salt and freshly ground black pepper*
**1 (¼-pound) store-cooked lobster, meat removed from shell (ask your fishseller to do this, if you like) and cut into small chunks, or 2½ cups cooked lobster meat**
**8 ounces crème fraîche**
**Grated zest of 4 lemons**

**1.** Bring a large pot of salted water to a boil. Meanwhile, cut the pasta sheets in 3½-inch squares; you should have about 20 squares.

**2.** Heat the corn oil in a large sauté pan until very hot. Add the bok choy, season with salt and pepper, and stir-fry until tender, about 1½ minutes.

**3.** Add the lobster to the pan, then stir in the crème fraîche and lemon zest.

**4.** Meanwhile, add the pasta squares to the boiling water and cook, stirring frequently, for about 1 minute, until tender. Drain.

**5.** Gently toss the pasta "handkerchiefs" with the lobster–bok choy sauce. Taste and adjust the seasoning if necessary. Serve immediately.

# WARM CHICKEN, FETA, AND MELON SEED PASTA SALAD

**Number of Servings: 4**  *Estimated Cost: $19*

1½ cups semi di melone pasta
1 rotisserie chicken (about 2 pounds)
10 ounces feta cheese, cubed or crumbled
½ cup thinly sliced drained hot cherry peppers
⅔ cup roughly torn fresh basil leaves
*½ cup extra virgin olive oil*
*Salt and freshly ground black pepper*

**1.** Bring a large pot of salted water to a boil. Add the pasta and cook according to the package instructions. Drain.

**2.** Meanwhile, remove the chicken skin and shred the meat into bite-size pieces. Place the chicken in a large bowl, along with all of its juices.

**3.** Add the pasta to the bowl. Add the feta, hot cherry peppers, basil leaves, and olive oil and toss. Season with salt and pepper, and serve warm.

# PIEROGI WITH HAM, DANDELION GREENS, AND SOUR CREAM MUSTARD SAUCE

**Number of Servings: 4**  *Estimated Cost: $17*

**24 store-bought potato and mushroom pierogi**
*1 tablespoon canola oil*
**4 cups trimmed dandelion greens**
**1¼ cups diced ham**
**⅓ cup Dijon mustard**
**1¼ cups sour cream**
*Salt and freshly ground black pepper*

**1.** Bring a large pot of salted water to a boil. Add the pierogi and cook according to the package instructions. Drain.

**2.** Meanwhile, heat the oil in a large sauté pan until hot. Add the dandelion greens and cook, stirring constantly, until wilted, about 1½ minutes. Add the ham, mustard, and sour cream. Cook until heated through; do not boil.

**3.** Add the pierogi to the pan and toss to coat. Season with salt and pepper if necessary, and serve.

# LINGUINE ALLA CARBONARA

**Number of Servings: 4**  *Estimated Cost: $14.50*

*1 tablespoon olive oil*
**8 ounces bacon, sliced crosswise into ⅓-inch-wide strips**
**1 medium-large onion, cut into small dice**
**14 ounces fresh linguine**
**6 egg yolks**
**1½ cups grated Parmigiano-Reggiano**
*Salt and freshly ground black pepper*

**1.** Bring a large pot of salted water to a boil.

**2.** Meanwhile, heat the olive oil in a very large sauté pan. Add the bacon and onion and cook, stirring frequently, for about 4 minutes, or until the onion is tender and the bacon is just beginning to color.

**3.** Add the linguine to the boiling water and cook according to package directions.

**4.** While the bacon and onion are cooking, gradually whisk 1 cup of the pasta cooking water into the egg yolks.

**5.** Drain the pasta and add it to the pan with the bacon and onion and stir well. Turn off the heat. Add the egg mixture and 1 cup of the Parmigiano to the pan. Toss to combine and coat the pasta thoroughly. The sauce will thicken as it rests. Season with salt and lots of freshly ground black pepper and transfer to a large serving bowl. Sprinkle the remaining Parmigiano on top of the pasta, and serve.

# SAUSAGE LASAGNA

**Number of Servings: 4** *Estimated Cost: $18*

**9 ounces fresh pasta sheets**
**1 (24-ounce) jar marinara sauce**
**8 cooked hot Italian sausages, cut into ½-inch slices**
**½ cup grated Parmigiano-Reggiano cheese**
*Salt and freshly ground black pepper*
**1 (12-ounce) package shredded whole-milk mozzarella (preferably low-moisture)**

**1.** Bring a large pot of salted water to a boil. Add the pasta sheets and cook for 1 minute. Drain and rinse with cold water to cool.

**2.** Spread one-quarter of the pasta sauce evenly over the bottom of a 15 x 10 ½-inch glass baking dish. Lay one-third of the sheets of pasta over the sauce, overlapping them only slightly if necessary. Spoon another one-quarter of the sauce on top of the pasta. Scatter half of the sausage slices over the sauce. Sprinkle half the Parmigiano evenly over the sausage. Repeat this process one more time. Arrange the remaining pasta on top and top with the remaining sauce. Season lightly with salt and pepper. Sprinkle the mozzarella over the top of the lasagna, covering it evenly.

**3.** Cover the lasagna tightly with plastic wrap. Microwave on high power for 4 minutes, or until the cheese is melted and the lasagna is hot throughout. Allow to sit for a minute before removing the plastic wrap, then cut into 4 rectangles and serve.

# Fish and Shellfish Main Dishes

# SOLE WITH CHARRED RED ONIONS AND LEMON BUTTER

**Number of Servings: 4**  *Estimated Cost: $18*

**4 small red onions, sliced into very thin rings**
*Salt and freshly ground black pepper*
*3½ sticks butter, cut into tablespoon-size chunks*
**Grated zest of 3 lemons plus ½ cup fresh lemon juice**
**4 sole fillets (about 1½ pounds total)**
**1 (⅔-ounce) package chives, chopped**

**1.** Preheat the broiler. Preheat a large sauté pan over medium heat.

**2.** Spread the onions on a baking sheet. Season with salt and pepper and dot with 4 tablespoons of the butter. Broil for 5 minutes, or until slightly charred and tender.

**3.** Meanwhile, in a small pot, bring the lemon zest and juice to a boil. Add 2 sticks of the butter; bring to a boil. Add the remaining stick and blend with an immersion blender until creamy and emulsified (or use a regular blender).

**4.** Add the lemon butter to the preheated pan and heat to just below a simmer, never to a boil. Season the sole with salt and pepper and add to the lemon butter. Cover and allow to poach for 3 minutes, or until just cooked through. Add the chives to the pan.

**5.** Mound a pile of onions on each plate and top with the sole. Spoon a generous amount of lemon butter on top and serve.

# PARMIGIANO FLOUNDER WITH WHITE BEANS AND OLIVE TAPENADE

**Number of Servings: 4**  *Estimated Cost: $19.25*

*Olive oil*
**4 flounder fillets (about 1¼ pounds total)**
*Salt and freshly ground black pepper*
**1 cup grated Parmigiano-Reggiano cheese**
**2½ (15-ounce) cans cannellini beans, drained**
**1¾ cups prepared marinara sauce**
**1 cup prepared tapenade**

**1.** Preheat the broiler. Line the broiler pan with aluminum foil and lightly coat with olive oil. Arrange the flounder fillets on the foil and season with salt and pepper. Sprinkle the top of the fillets generously with the Parmigiano, coating them thoroughly.

**2.** Place the fish under the broiler and broil for 3 to 5 minutes, depending on the thickness of the fillets; the cheese should bubble and turn golden brown.

**3.** Meanwhile, in a large sauté pan heat the beans, marinara sauce, and tapenade over high heat until hot. Season with salt and pepper if necessary.

**4.** To serve, divide the beans among four large bowls, and lay the flounder on top of the beans.

# SEA BASS WITH LEEKS, CHESTNUTS, AND DATES

**Number of Servings: 4**  *Estimated Cost: $20*

*3 tablespoons butter*
**4 medium leeks, washed and sliced thinly on the diagonal**
**1 (15-ounce) can chestnuts in syrup, drained, liquid reserved, and chopped**
**½ cup chopped dates**
*2 tablespoons cider vinegar*
*1 cup water*
*Salt and freshly ground black pepper*
**1¼ pounds sea bass fillets, sliced diagonally into 12 thin medallions**

**1.** Heat the butter in a large sauté pan until hot but not smoking. Add the leeks and cook for about 2 minutes, or until they are nearly tender.

**2.** Add the chestnuts, dates, vinegar, and water and bring to a boil. Season with salt and pepper and lower the heat to a simmer. Season the sea bass with salt and pepper and add to the pan. Cover and simmer for about 2 minutes, or until the fish is just cooked through.

**3.** Arrange the fish on four plates and spoon the sauce over. Serve hot.

# COD FLASH-FRY WITH MINT

**Number of Servings: 4**  *Estimated Cost: $17.75*

*2 quarts canola oil*
*Flour for dredging*
*Salt and freshly ground black pepper*
**4 eggs**
**1 pound cod fillet, cut into 1-inch chunks**
**2 large Vidalia onions, cut into ½-inch rings**
**1 cup prepared General Tso's sauce**
**⅓ cup chopped fresh mint**

**1.** In a large pot, heat the oil until very hot but not smoking, about 400 degrees.

**2.** Meanwhile, spread the flour on a plate and season with salt and pepper. Beat the eggs in a shallow bowl. Separate the Vidalia rings, and dredge the cod and onions in the flour, then dip in the eggs to coat. Add the cod and onions to the oil, being careful that they do not clump together. Cook for about 5 minutes, stirring frequently, until golden brown. Drain on paper towels and season with salt and pepper.

**3.** In a large bowl, toss the cod and onions with the sauce and mint. Serve immediately.

# COD PROVENÇAL

**Number of Servings: 4**  *Estimated Cost: $15.25*

1 (20-ounce) can whole plum tomatoes in puree
4 thin cod fillets (about 1½ pounds total), cut crosswise into 3-inch-wide pieces
*Salt and freshly ground black pepper*
1½ cups bread crumbs
*6 tablespoons olive oil*
2 cloves garlic, chopped
2 tablespoons chopped fresh oregano

**1.** Preheat the oven to 500 degrees.

**2.** Meanwhile, remove the tomatoes from the puree and coarsely chop them. Mix back into the puree, then spread on a foil-lined baking pan. Season the cod with salt and pepper and arrange on top of the sauce.

**3.** In a small bowl, mix the bread crumbs with the olive oil, garlic, and oregano. Season with salt and pepper. Cover the cod evenly with this mixture and place in the oven.

**4.** Bake for 3½ minutes. Turn on the broiler and broil until the fish is just cooked through and the bread crumbs are golden brown. Serve hot.

# RED, WHITE, AND GREEN COD

**Number of Servings: 4**  *Estimated Cost: $20.25*

*3 tablespoons extra virgin olive oil*
**4 cloves garlic, crushed**
**1½ pounds cod fillet, cut into 1-inch chunks**
*Salt and freshly ground black pepper*
**1 (14½-ounce) large can lentil soup, about 2 cups**
**1 (7-ounce) jar pimientos, drained and cut into strips**
**¼ cup chopped flat-leaf fresh parsley**

**1.** In a large sauté pan, heat the oil until hot but not smoking. Add the garlic and sauté until it begins to turn golden.

**2.** Season the cod with salt and pepper and add to the pan. When the cod chunks begin to brown on the first side, flip them and add the lentil soup and pimientos to the pan. Bring to a simmer and cook just until the fish is cooked through. Adjust the seasoning and serve, sprinkling the parsley on top.

# TROUT WITH BUTTERNUT SQUASH AND BLOOD ORANGES

**Number of Servings: 4**  *Estimated Cost: $20*

**6 small blood or navel oranges**
*6 tablespoons butter*
*Salt and freshly ground black pepper*
**1 (12-ounce) package frozen butternut squash puree**
*2 tablespoons canola oil*
**4 rainbow trout fillets (about 6 ounces each), skin on**

**1.** With a sharp knife, remove the peel and white pith from 4 of the oranges. Working over a bowl to catch the juice, separate the oranges into segments. Set the segments aside, and reserve the juice. Squeeze the juice from the remaining 2 oranges and combine with the reserved juice.

**2.** Heat a very large straight-sided sauté pan over high heat. Add the orange juice and bring to a simmer. Simmer rapidly to reduce the juice until thick and syrupy, about 3 minutes.

**3.** Add the butter and swirl the pan to blend the butter with the juice. Add the orange segments and season lightly with salt. Lower the heat to keep the mixture warm.

**4.** Meanwhile, microwave the butternut puree for 5 minutes, or according to the package instructions; keep warm.

**5.** Heat the oil in a large sauté pan over high heat. Season the trout with salt and pepper. Place skin side down in the pan and cook for about 3½ minutes, or until the skin is crisp and golden. Turn and continue to cook for another 1½ minutes.

**6.** To serve, make a mound of one-quarter of the squash puree in the center of each plate. Top with the trout and spoon the orange sauce and segments over all.

# CORNMEAL AND RED ONION-CRUSTED SKATE WITH LIME BUTTER

**Number of Servings: 4**  *Estimated Cost: $17*

*⅔ cup corn oil*
**4 (5- to 6-ounce) pieces skinless skate fillet**
**2 egg whites, beaten**
**2 small red onions, thinly sliced**
*Salt and freshly ground black pepper*
*1 cup yellow cornmeal*
*8 tablespoons (1 stick) butter*
**6 tablespoons fresh lime juice**

**1.** Heat ⅓ cup of the oil in each of two large sauté pans until very hot.

**2.** Meanwhile, lay the skate on a work surface. Brush the tops with egg white and layer the onion slices on top of the skate to cover it completely. Brush gently with egg white again and season with salt and pepper. Sprinkle liberally with the cornmeal to coat the top of the fish.

**3.** Gently shake the fillets to remove excess cornmeal and carefully place, onion side down, in the hot oil. Cook until the cornmeal begins to turn golden brown.

**4.** Holding the skate with a spatula, drain the oil from each pan. Add 4 tablespoons of the butter to each pan. Cook over medium heat until the butter turns brown. Turn the skate and cook for 30 seconds on the other side.

**5.** Turn off the heat. Transfer the fish to serving plates, and add 3 tablespoons of the lime juice to each pan. Stir well; season the lime butter with salt and pepper. Serve the skate with the lime butter spooned around and over it.

# BLACK-AND-TAN SALMON WITH SCALLIONS

**Number of Servings: 4**  *Estimated Cost: $13.50*

*2 tablespoons corn oil*
**1½ pounds skinless salmon fillet, cut into 4 portions**
*Salt and freshly ground black pepper*
**2 large (14½-ounce) cans black bean soup, about 4 cups**
**Grated zest of 1 large lime, plus 1 tablespoon fresh lime juice**
**¼ cup prepared sweet mango chutney**
**1 bunch scallions, sliced**

**1.** Heat the oil in a large sauté pan over high heat until very hot.

**2.** Season the salmon on both sides with salt and pepper and place it in the pan. Cook for about 3 minutes, or until it is a beautiful golden brown on the first side.

**3.** Meanwhile, in a medium bowl, combine the soup, lime zest and juice, and chutney.

**4.** When the the salmon is browned, flip it over and add the soup mixture to the pan. Simmer for about 2 minutes for medium, or until the salmon is cooked to the desired doneness. Season with salt and pepper if necessary, sprinkle with the scallions, and serve.

# HONEY-GLAZED SALMON WITH CINNAMON, CARROTS, AND CHICORY

**Number of Servings: 4**  *Estimated Cost: $16.75*

**4 thin skinless salmon fillets (about 1½ pounds total)**
*Salt and freshly ground black pepper*
**1 teaspoon ground cinnamon**
**½ cup honey**
*3 tablespoons corn oil*
**4 carrots, peeled and thinly sliced**
**5 cups chicory or curly endive, thinly sliced**
*2 tablespoons white vinegar*

**1.** Preheat the broiler. Season the salmon with salt and pepper and place on the broiling pan.

**2.** In a small bowl, mix the cinnamon and honey. Lightly coat the salmon with this mixture; reserve the remainder. Broil the salmon for 5 minutes, or until lightly charred. Keep warm.

**3.** Meanwhile, heat the oil in a large sauté pan until hot but not smoking. Add the carrots to the hot oil and cook for about 2 minutes, stirring frequently. Add the chicory and season with salt and pepper. Cook until the chicory is wilted and tender.

**4.** Add the vinegar and the reserved honey mixture to the pan and toss to coat the carrots and chicory.

**5.** Arrange the bed of carrot-chicory mixture on each plate, and serve the salmon on top.

# SALMON IN BUTTERNUT SQUASH BARBECUE SAUCE

**Number of Servings: 4**  *Estimated Cost: $18*

**3 small red onions, cut into ⅕-inch-thick rings**
*Salt and freshly ground black pepper*
*4 tablespoons butter, cut into small chunks*
**2 (16-ounce) cans butternut squash soup**
**⅓ cup barbecue sauce**
**1½ pounds skinless salmon fillet, cut into 12 thin slices**

**1.** Preheat the broiler. Spread the onions on the broiler pan, season with salt and pepper, and dot with the butter. Broil until charred and tender, about 5 minutes.

**2.** Meanwhile, bring the soup and the barbecue sauce to a boil in a large sauté pan. Season the salmon well with salt and pepper. Reduce the heat under the soup and gently place the salmon in the pan. Shake the pan to submerge the fish completely. Cover and cook, keeping the soup just under the simmering point, for about 5 minutes, until the salmon is just cooked through.

**3.** To serve, pile the onions in the bottom of four large bowls. Top each pile with 3 salmon slices and ladle the soup over the fish.

# SALMON WITH SHIITAKE MUSHROOMS IN GINGER-SOY BROTH

**Number of Servings: 4**  *Estimated Cost: $20*

**1 (2-inch) piece ginger, pushed through a garlic press, smashed, or grated fine**
**1 small head Napa cabbage, quartered and sliced crosswise**
**7 ounces shiitake mushrooms, sliced**
*Salt and freshly ground black pepper*
**⅓ cup tamari soy sauce**
*1 tablespoon sugar*
*1 tablespoon white vinegar*
*1 cup water*
**1¼ to 1½ pounds skinless salmon fillet, cut on a diagonal into slices about ¾ inch thick**

**1.** Heat a very large sauté pan until smoking. Add the ginger and stir-fry for about 30 seconds. Add the cabbage and shiitakes, season lightly with salt and pepper, and stir-fry until wilted. Add the soy sauce, sugar, vinegar, and water and bring to a simmer.

**2.** Season the salmon with salt and pepper. Add to the pan, submerging the salmon pieces in the broth as much as possible. Cover the pan, reduce the heat, and cook very gently, just below a simmer, for 2 minutes, or until the salmon is just cooked through. Adjust the seasoning.

**3.** Ladle the salmon and broth into bowls and serve.

# SEARED SALMON WITH SUGAR SNAP PEAS AND HERRING

**Number of Servings: 4** *Estimated Cost: $15.75*

**1 (16-ounce) jar herring in sour cream**
*3 tablespoons corn oil*
**4 skinless salmon fillets (about 1½ pounds total)**
*Salt and freshly ground black pepper*
**8 ounces sugar snap peas**
**1 bunch scallions, sliced diagonally**

**1.** Microwave the herring for about 3 minutes, stirring gently midway. Keep warm.

**2.** Meanwhile, put 2 tablespoons of the oil in one large sauté pan, put the remaining 1 tablespoon oil in another large sauté pan, and heat until hot.

**3.** Season the salmon with salt and pepper and place in the pan containing 2 table-spoons oil. Cook until golden brown on one side, about 2½ minutes; turn and cook for 2½ minutes more, or until just cooked through. Remove from the pan and set aside.

**4.** Meanwhile, add the sugar snap peas to the other pan and sauté for 2 to 3 minutes, or until tender but slightly crunchy. Season with salt and pepper. Add the hot herring to the pan and toss gently to combine.

**5.** Arrange a bed of the herring mixture on each plate. Top with the salmon, sprinkle with the scallions, and serve hot.

# MAHI-MAHI WITH ENDIVE AND ORANGE MARMALADE GLAZE

**Number of Servings: 4**  *Estimated Cost: $19.25*

½ **cup orange marmalade**
*3 tablespoons sherry vinegar*
**4 thin mahi-mahi fillets (about 1¼ pounds total)**
*Salt and freshly ground black pepper*
*3 tablespoons olive oil*
**1 teaspoon chopped fresh tarragon**
**4 medium endive, sliced (about 5 cups)**

**1.** Preheat the broiler. Mix together the orange marmalade and 2 tablespoons of the sherry vinegar. Season the mahi-mahi with salt and pepper, and arrange on the broiling rack. Coat liberally with the marmalade glaze.

**2.** Broil the fish for 5 minutes, or until it is cooked through and the glaze begins to char.

**3.** Meanwhile, mix together the remaining 1 tablespoon sherry vinegar, the olive oil, and the tarragon in a medium bowl. Add the endive and toss to coat. Season with salt and pepper.

**4.** Make a bed of endive on each of four plates. Place the mahi-mahi on top of the endive and serve.

# GRILLED SQUID WITH COCONUT BROTH, LEEKS, AND PAPAYA

**Number of Servings: 4**  *Estimated Cost: $20*

1¾ **pounds squid, cleaned and sliced**
*¼ cup corn oil*
3 **large leeks, washed and cut diagonally into thick slices**
*Salt and freshly ground black pepper*
2 **(14-ounce) cans coconut ginger soup**
2 **small or 1 large ripe papaya, peeled, cut in half, seeded, and thinly sliced crosswise**
⅓ **cup chopped fresh cilantro**

**1.** Heat a grill pan under a hot broiler.

**2.** Meanwhile, in a medium bowl, gently toss the squid with 2 tablespoons of the oil to coat. In another medium bowl, gently toss the leeks with the remaining 2 tablespoons oil to coat; be careful not to separate the leek rings. Season the squid and leeks with salt and pepper.

**3.** Place the squid and leeks in the grill pan and broil for 3 to 5 minutes, or until the squid is just cooked through and the leeks are tender and slightly charred. The squid may be done before the leeks, so remove it from the pan as you see it cook through.

**4.** Meanwhile, in a medium pot, heat the soup until boiling.

**5.** Place the leeks in the center of four bowls. Layer the papaya slices on top, followed by the squid. Ladle the soup into each bowl, sprinkle with the cilantro, and serve hot.

# SAVORY SEAFOOD STEW

**Number of Servings: 4** *Estimated Cost: $18.50*

*¼ cup extra virgin olive oil*
**1½ cups zucchini cut into ½-inch half-moons**
**1 to 1¼ pounds lemon sole, cut into 1-inch chunks**
*Salt and freshly ground black pepper*
**2 cups store-bought precooked cubed golden potatoes**
**¼ cup chopped fresh savory, marjoram, or oregano**
**1 (24-ounce) jar Fra Diavolo Sauce**

**1.** Heat the olive oil in a large sauté pan until hot but not smoking. Add the zucchini and cook for 45 seconds, stirring frequently.

**2.** Season the lemon sole with salt and pepper and add to the pan. Cook for about 1 minute. Add the potatoes, savory, and sauce, cover, and bring to a boil, Lower the heat to a simmer. Simmer for about 2½ minutes, or until the sole is cooked through and potatoes are hot.

**3.** Transfer the stew to shallow bowls. Serve hot.

Capellini with Littleneck Clams (page 136)

Sautéed Pork with Snow Peas, Walnuts, and Beets (page 240)

Hot-and-Sour Shrimp
Rice Noodle Soup (page 69)

12 Eggs in a Pan (page 230)

Ham on Rye with Artichokes and Dijon (page 102)

Roast Beef and
Boursin Panini (page 108)

Black-and-Tan Salmon with Scallions
(page 165)

Shrimp and Noodle Saté Sauté (page 183)

Warm Chicken, Feta, and
Melon Seed Pasta Salad
(page 142)

Beef Curry Sauté (page 217)

Mushroom and Red Onion Burger (page 100)

Gnocchi with Toasted Garlic, Walnuts,
and Bitter Greens (page 135)

Goat Cheese, Radish, and Dried
Cranberry Salad (page 78)

Warm Brownies with a
Salty Peanut Sauce (page 276)

Pretty Peach Melba (page 261)

Pineapple French Toast (page 273)

# CATFISH AND RICE SOFRITO

**Number of Servings: 4** *Estimated Cost: $13.50*

*¼ cup corn oil*
**4 thin catfish fillets (about 1¾ pounds total)**
*Salt and freshly ground black pepper*
*Wondra flour for dusting*
*2 tablespoons butter*
*2 cups water*
**2½ cups instant rice**
**1 medium red onion, thinly sliced**
*¼ cup red wine vinegar*
**1 cup Goya Sofrito**

**1.** Heat the oil in a very large sauté pan until hot. Season the catfish fillets with salt and pepper and dust the tops with flour. Arrange floured side down in the pan and cook for about 2½ minutes, or until golden brown. Add the butter and cook for 1 minute. Turn the fillets and cook for 1½ minutes, or until just cooked through. Transfer to a plate.

**2.** Meanwhile, in a medium saucepan, bring the water to a boil. Season lightly with salt, stir in the rice, and cover tightly. Turn off heat and allow the rice to stand for 5 minutes.

**3.** In a medium bowl, combine the red onion and red wine vinegar. Season with salt and pepper and set aside to marinate. Drain before using.

**4.** Stir the sofrito into the rice. Taste, and season with salt and pepper if necessary.

**5.** To serve, place a pile of rice in the center of each plate, top with the drained onions, and place a catfish fillet on top of the onions.

# CLAM BRODETTATTO WITH CHORIZO AND PEAS

**Number of Servings: 4**  *Estimated Cost: $14.25*

*2 tablespoons extra virgin olive oil*
**4 ounces Spanish-style chorizo sausage, sliced**
**½ cup dry white wine**
*¼ cup water*
**1 large pinch saffron threads**
**2 pounds littleneck clams, scrubbed**
**1 cup frozen peas**

**1.** In a large sauté pan, heat the olive oil until hot but not smoking. Add the chorizo and stir. Pour the wine and water into the pan, add the saffron, and bring to a rapid boil over high heat. Add the clams to the pan, immediately cover, and cook for about 1 minute.

**2.** Add the peas and continue to cook until the clams just open and the peas are hot; be careful not to overcook the clams, as they'll become rubbery. Discard any clams that did not open.

**3.** Spoon the clams and broth into four bowls and serve immediately. Or serve the clams over a bed of rice.

# CURRIED MUSSEL FRICASSEE

**Number of Servings: 4**  *Estimated Cost: $15.25*

**2 large flatbreads or pitas**
*1 tablespoon canola oil*
**1 tablespoon prepared Thai hot curry paste**
**1 (14-ounce) can coconut milk**
**3 pounds mussels, scrubbed and debearded**
**12 ounces prepared pico de gallo or other fresh salsa**
*Salt and freshly ground black pepper*

**1.** Preheat a grill pan until very hot.

**2.** Grill the flatbreads, turning once, until they have grill marks on both sides. Set aside.

**3.** Meanwhile, heat the oil in a large pot. Add the curry paste and stir to break it up. Add the coconut milk and bring to a boil. Add the mussels to the pot and cover tightly. After about 1 minute, add the pico de gallo to the pot and stir to combine. Cover and cook for about 1 minute more, or until the mussels have opened. Discard any mussels that did not open, and season with salt and pepper.

**4.** Divide the mussels and broth among four large bowls, and serve with the grilled flatbread.

# CRAB CAKES WITH AVOCADO DIP AND ARUGULA SALAD

**Number of Servings: 4**  *Estimated Cost: $20*

*½ cup canola oil*
**1 pound jumbo lump crabmeat, picked through for shells and cartilage**
**Grated zest of 4 large lemons plus 3 tablespoons fresh lemon juice**
**⅔ cup mayonnaise**
*Salt and freshly ground black pepper*
*Flour for dredging*
*2 tablespoons extra virgin olive oil*
**7 ounces baby arugula**
**1 cup prepared avocado dip**

**1.** Heat the canola oil in a very large sauté pan over high heat.

**2.** Meanwhile, in a large bowl, thoroughly combine the crabmeat, lemon zest, 1 tablespoon of the lemon juice, and the mayonnaise. Season well with salt and pepper. Divide the mixture into 8 equal portions and form each one into a patty about ¾ inch thick.

**3.** Spread the flour on a plate and season with salt and pepper. Gently dredge the patties in the flour and place them in the sauté pan. Cook for 2½ minutes per side, or until golden brown and hot throughout. Drain on paper towels.

**4.** Meanwhile, combine the remaining 2 tablespoons lemon juice with the olive oil. Toss the arugula gently with the lemon dressing, and season with salt and pepper.

**5.** To serve, divide the avocado dip among four small ramekins or cups. Place 2 crab cakes on each plate and place a pile of arugula salad next to them. Serve with the ramekins

# SAUTÉED SCALLOPS WITH PICKLED GINGER RED CABBAGE

**Number of Servings: 4**  *Estimated Cost: $20*

*½ cup corn oil*
**4 prepared zucchini cakes**
**12 large sea scallops (about 1 pound)**
*Salt and freshly ground black pepper*
**2 bunches scallions, cut diagonally into 2-inch pieces**
**¼ cup pickled ginger**
**1 (16-ounce) jar sweet-and-sour red cabbage**

**1.** Heat 3 tablespoons of the oil in a large sauté pan until very hot. Heat the remaining 5 tablespoons oil in another large sauté pan until hot. Place the zucchini cakes in the second pan and sauté until crisp on both sides, about 1 minute per side. Drain on paper towels; keep warm.

**2.** Meanwhile, season the scallops well with salt and pepper. Place in the first pan and cook until golden brown on the first side. Turn and continue to cook for another minute, then remove to a plate.

**3.** Add the scallions to the pan and stir-fry until almost tender. Add the ginger and cabbage and bring to a simmer. Taste and season with salt and pepper.

**4.** To serve, make a bed of red cabbage on each plate. Top each with a zucchini cake and 3 scallops.

# SHRIMP AND BROCCOLI FLASH-FRY

**Number of Servings: 4**  *Estimated Cost: $19.50*

*2 quarts corn oil*
*Flour for dredging*
**4 eggs**
**1½ pounds large shrimp (20 to 25 count), peeled and deveined**
**4 cups large broccoli florets**
*Salt and freshly ground black pepper*
**1¼ cups prepared sweet ginger sesame sauce**
**⅓ cup chopped fresh cilantro**

**1.** Heat the oil in a large pot until very hot but not smoking, about 400 degrees.

**2.** Spread the flour on a plate. Beat the eggs in a shallow bowl. Dredge the shrimp and broccoli in the flour, then in the eggs to coat, and add to the oil, being careful to separate any pieces that stick together. Fry for 5 minutes, or until golden brown. Drain on paper towels.

**3.** Season the shrimp and broccoli well with salt and pepper. In a large bowl, toss with the sauce and cilantro. Serve hot.

# SHRIMP AND SCALLION FRITTATA

**Number of Servings: 4** *Estimated Cost: $13*

¼ *cup corn oil*
**1½ pounds shrimp (31 to 40 count), peeled, split down the back, and deveined**
*Salt and freshly ground black pepper*
**2 bunches scallions, thinly sliced on the diagonal**
**9 eggs**
**3 tablespoons mirin (rice wine)**

**1.** Preheat the oven to 500 degrees.

**2.** Heat the corn oil in a large sauté pan until hot. Season the shrimp with salt and pepper. Add the scallions and shrimp to the pan, stir, and cook until the shrimp are translucent pink and nearly cooked through.

**3.** Meanwhile, beat the eggs in a medium bowl. Stir in the mirin, season with salt and pepper, and add to the pan. Continue to stir until large curds form; the eggs should still be wet. Smooth the top of the frittata.

**4.** Place the pan in the oven and bake for 1 to 2 more minutes, until the eggs are set.

**5.** Remove from the oven and loosen the sides with a rubber spatula. Invert the frittata onto a plate or cutting board, cut into wedges, and serve.

# SHRIMP FRA DIAVOLO WITH COUSCOUS AND BROCCOLI RABE

**Number of Servings: 4**  *Estimated Cost: $18*

*3 cups water*
**2 (6.1-ounce) packages tomato-lentil couscous or other flavored couscous**
*3 tablespoons olive oil*
**1½ pounds shrimp (36 to 40 count), peeled and deveined**
*Salt and freshly ground black pepper*
**1 bunch broccoli rabe, cut into 2-inch pieces (about 3 cups)**
**2 tablespoons chili paste**
**Grated zest and juice of 1 lemon**

**1.** Bring the water to a boil in a medium pot. Add the couscous and flavor packet. Cook according to package instructions.

**2.** Meanwhile, in a large pot, heat 2 tablespoons of the olive oil until very hot. Season the shrimp with salt and pepper and add to the pot. After about 1 minute, add the broccoli rabe, cover, and cook, stirring occasionally, until the shrimp are fully cooked and the broccoli rabe is tender, about 3 minutes. Remove from the heat.

**3.** Fluff the couscous with a fork. Transfer to a large bowl, add the shrimp mixture, the remaining 1 tablespoon olive oil, the chili paste, and lemon zest and juice, and toss to mix. Season with salt and pepper, if necessary, and serve.

# SHRIMP AND NOODLE SATÉ SAUTÉ

**Number of Servings: 4** *Estimated Cost: $19.25*

1 (8-ounce) package thin rice noodles
*¼ cup corn oil*
3 slices bacon, cut crosswise into thin strips
1¼ pounds shrimp (36 to 40 count), peeled and deveined
*Salt and freshly ground black pepper*
4 cups tightly packed bite-size pieces kale
2 (7-ounce) jars Thai peanut sauce
*½ cup water*

**1.** Place the rice noodles in a large bowl and cover with warm water. Soak for 30 minutes. Drain.

**2.** Heat the oil in a large sauté pan until hot but not smoking. Add the bacon and cook, stirring frequently, until it begins to brown.

**3.** Season the shrimp with salt and pepper and add to the pan. After about 1 minute, stir the shrimp and add the kale. Stir, cover, and cook until the kale begins to wilt. Add the rice noodles, cover, and cook until tender.

**4.** Add the saté sauce and water and bring to a simmer. Season with salt and pepper if necessary, and toss to evenly coat all the noodles. Serve hot.

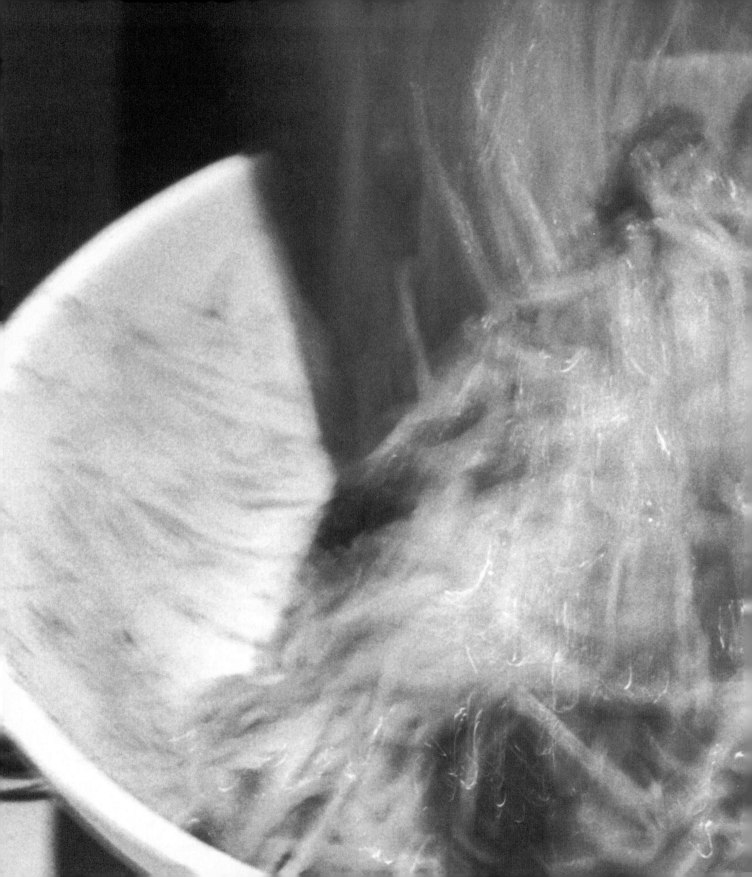

# SHRIMP SCAMPI WITH GRILLED BREAD

**Number of Servings: 4** *Estimated Cost: $20*

**6 cloves garlic, peeled, 2 cloves left whole, 4 cloves thinly sliced**
**²/₃ ciabatta, cut into 4 rectangles**
*²/₃ cup extra virgin olive oil*
*Salt and freshly ground black pepper*
*4 tablespoons butter*
**1½ pounds shrimp (16 to 20 count), peeled and deveined**
**Juice of 3 lemons**
**⅓ cup flat-leaf chopped parsley**

**1.** Heat a grill pan until very hot.

**2.** Rub 2 of the garlic cloves onto both sides of the bread to flavor it. Brush the bread with 2 tablespoons of the olive oil and season with salt and pepper. Grill, turning once, until slightly charred and crunchy on both sides. Set aside.

**3.** Meanwhile, in a large sauté pan, heat the butter and the remaining olive oil. Add the 4 sliced garlic cloves and cook for about 30 seconds; do not allow to brown. Season the shrimp with salt and pepper and add to the pan. Cook for about 1½ minutes, then stir the shrimp and add the lemon juice. Simmer until the shrimp are just cooked through, about 1½ more minutes. Add the parsley, and season the sauce if necessary.

**4.** To serve, place a slice of grilled bread on each of four plates. Divide the shrimp evenly among the bread, and generously spoon the sauce on top.

# SKEWERED SHRIMP WITH BEANS AND SCALLIONS

**Number of Servings: 4** *Estimated Cost: $20*

1½ pounds large shrimp (20 to 25 count), peeled and deveined
½ cup plus 3 tablespoons prepared garlic rib sauce
*Salt and freshly ground black pepper*
*1 tablespoon corn oil*
2 cloves garlic, chopped
2 (14-ounce) cans cannellini beans, drained
1 large bunch scallions, sliced

**1.** Put 8 bamboo skewers in water to soak for an hour.

**2.** Preheat a grill pan until very hot.

**3.** Skewer the shrimp, about 3 per skewer. Brush the shrimp with 3 tablespoons of the garlic rib sauce. Season with salt and pepper. Grill 1½ to 2 minutes per side, or until the shrimp are just done.

**4.** Meanwhile, heat the oil in a large sauté pan until hot. Add the garlic and sauté until fragrant, about 45 seconds. Add the beans and the remaining ½ cup rib sauce. Simmer until heated through.

**5.** To serve, spoon one-quarter of the bean mixture onto each plate. Lay 2 skewers of shrimp across the top, scatter the scallions over the shrimp and beans, and serve.

# Poultry Main Dishes

# CHICKEN AND CAULIFLOWER FLASH-FRY

**Number of Servings: 4**  *Estimated Cost: $19.75*

*2 quarts corn or canola oil*
*Flour for dredging*
*Salt and freshly ground black pepper*
**4 eggs**
**1 large head cauliflower, cut into medium florets**
**1½ pounds boneless, skinless chicken breasts, cut into 1-inch chunks**
**1 (8-ounce) jar pad Thai sauce**
**½ cup torn fresh basil leaves**

**1.** In a large pot, heat the oil until very hot but not smoking, about 400 degrees.

**2.** Meanwhile, spread the flour on a plate and season with salt and pepper. Beat the eggs in a shallow bowl.

**3.** Dredge the cauliflower and chicken in the flour, then dip in the eggs to coat. Carefully add the cauliflower and chicken to the hot oil, stirring to prevent sticking. Fry until golden brown and cooked through, about 5 minutes. Drain on paper towels and season with salt and pepper.

**4.** Place the cauliflower and chicken in a large bowl. Add the pad Thai sauce and basil and toss well. Serve immediately.

# CHICKEN AND WILD MUSHROOM STRUDEL

**Number of Servings: 4** *Estimated Cost: $20*

**8 sheets frozen phyllo, at room temperature**
**3 tablespoons fresh thyme leaves**
*12 tablespoons (1½ sticks) butter, 6 tablespoons melted*
**1 pound mixed wild mushrooms, sliced**
**1 rotisserie chicken (about 2 pounds), skin removed and meat shredded**
**1¼ cups sour cream**
*Salt and freshly ground black pepper*

**1.** Preheat the oven to 450 degrees and heat a large sauté pan over high heat.

**2.** Lay 1 phyllo sheet on a work surface (cover the remaining sheets with a damp towel). Reserve 1 tablespoon of the thyme. Brush the sheet generously with the melted butter and sprinkle with thyme leaves. Repeat the layering until you have a stack of 4 sheets of phyllo; place on a parchment-lined baking sheet. Repeat so that you have another stack of 4 sheets of phyllo; place on another parchment-lined baking sheet.

**3.** Bake the phyllo stacks for 5 minutes, or until golden brown and crisp.

**4.** Meanwhile, add the remaining butter to the pan. Add the reserved thyme and the mushrooms. Cook until the mushrooms are tender and slightly brown. Add the chicken and cook until very hot. Mix in the sour cream and season well with salt and pepper.

**5.** To serve, break the phyllo stacks into 12 pieces. Make a stack on each plate, using 3 pieces of phyllo for each serving, alternating the chicken mixture with the phyllo.

# CHICKEN WITH TOMATO, BASIL, AND CRISPY PARMIGIANO CRACKERS

**Number of Servings: 4**   *Estimated Cost: $13.50*

¼ **cup grated Parmigiano-Reggiano cheese**
*⅓ cup plus 2 tablespoons extra virgin olive oil*
1½ **pounds thin-cut chicken cutlets**
*Salt and freshly ground black pepper*
**7 large cloves garlic, chopped**
**1 (28-ounce) can San Marzano whole peeled tomatoes, drained, ½ cup liquid reserved**
**24 fresh basil leaves, torn into small pieces**

**1.** Spray four ovenproof dinner plates with 7-inch "faces" with cooking spray. Sprinkle 2 table-spoons of the grated Parmigiano evenly over each plate. Microwave each for 2 minutes; the cheese should be completely melted and beginning to turn a pale golden brown. Cool for about 45 seconds, loosen the edges of each cheese disk (fricco) with a thin spatula, then grab an edge and carefully peel the cracker from the plate. Set aside to cool and harden.

**2.** Heat 2 tablespoons of the oil in a 14-inch sauté pan over medium-low heat. Season the chicken with salt and pepper and add to the pan; the oil should barely bubble. Cook slowly for 2½ minutes, then flip the chicken.

**3.** Meanwhile, heat remaining ⅓ cup olive oil in a large sauté pan over medium-high heat. Add the garlic and cook, stirring frequently, until lightly golden. Add the tomatoes and cook for about 3 minutes, stirring often. Add the reserved tomato liquid and bring to a simmer. Season with salt and pepper and stir in the basil leaves.

**4.** Pour the sauce over the chicken in the pan and shake to coat the chicken evenly. Turn up the heat and bring to a simmer. Divide the chicken and sauce among four large wide bowls. Break each cracker in half, and lay across the chicken. Serve immediately.

# CHICKEN WITH LEMON, CAPERS, AND RED ONIONS

**Number of Servings: 4**  *Estimated Cost: $12.75*

12 tablespoons (1½ sticks) butter, at room temperature
*Flour for dredging*
*Salt and freshly ground black pepper*
**2 eggs**
**4 thin chicken cutlets (about 5 ounces each)**
**½ cup lemon juice**
**2 ounces capers, chopped**
**½ cup diced red onion**

**1.** Heat 4 tablespoons of the butter in a large sauté pan over medium-low heat until hot and lightly foaming but not brown.

**2.** Meanwhile, spread the flour on a plate and season with salt and pepper. Beat the eggs in a shallow dish. Dredge the chicken in the flour and then dip in the eggs to coat.

**3.** Add the chicken to the hot butter and cook, turning once, until light golden brown on both sides and cooked through, about 2 minutes per side. Transfer the chicken to a platter and season with salt and pepper.

**4.** While the chicken is cooking, bring the lemon juice to a boil in another large sauté pan. Whisk in the remaining 8 tablespoons butter and simmer until the sauce is slightly reduced. Add the capers and season the sauce with salt, if necessary, and pepper.

**5.** Pour the sauce over the chicken and sprinkle with the red onion. Serve immediately.

# GOLDEN CHICKEN AND TALEGGIO CUTLETS

**Number of Servings: 4**  *Estimated Cost: $17.75*

*1 cup canola oil*
*Fine cornmeal for dredging*
**3 eggs**
*Salt and freshly ground black pepper*
**4 thin chicken cutlets (about 1¼ pounds total)**
**¾ pound Taleggio cheese, cut into thin slices**
*1 tablespoon plus 2 teaspoons sherry vinegar*
*2 tablespoons extra virgin olive oil*
**1 (7-ounce) package baby arugula**

**1.** Heat ½ cup of the canola oil in each of two large sauté pans.

**2.** Meanwhile, spread the cornmeal on a plate. Beat the eggs in a shallow dish.

**3.** Season the chicken cutlets with salt and pepper. Press a cheese slice firmly on top of each cutlet, covering it. Dredge the cutlets in the cornmeal, then dip into the eggs to coat, and then dredge again in the cornmeal.

**4.** Once the oil is hot, place 2 cutlets cheese side down in each pan. Cook for about 2 minutes, turn, and cook for 3 minutes on the other side. The chicken should be golden brown, crispy, and cooked through and the cheese completely melted.

**5.** Combine the sherry vinegar with the olive oil. Toss with the arugula in a bowl. Season the salad with salt and pepper, and serve a small pile along with each chicken cutlet.

# PARMIGIANO CHICKEN WITH MOLTEN PROVOLONE

**Number of Servings: 4**  *Estimated Cost: $17.25*

*¾ cup corn oil*
*⅓ cup garlic oil*
*1½ cups fine cornmeal*
**1 cup grated Parmigiano-Reggiano cheese**
**3 eggs**
**4 thin chicken breast cutlets (about 1¼ pounds total)**
*Salt and freshly ground black pepper*
**8 ounces sliced provolone**
**1½ bunches broccoli rabe, washed and cut into 2-inch pieces**

**1.** Put the corn oil in one large sauté pan, the garlic oil in another large sauté pan, and heat over medium heat.

**2.** Meanwhile, in a shallow bowl, mix ¾ cup of the cornmeal with the Parmigiano. Spread the remaining ¾ cup cornmeal on a plate. Beat the eggs in a shallow bowl.

**3.** Season the chicken breasts with salt and pepper. Arrange one-quarter of the slices of provolone on each chicken breast, and press the cheese firmly onto the cutlets. Dredge the chicken in the plain cornmeal, dip in the egg to coat, and dredge thoroughly in the cheese and cornmeal mixture. Place cheese side down in the pan with the corn oil and cook until golden brown on the first side. Turn the chicken and cook for another 3 minutes, or until the outside is crisp and golden, the cheese is melted, and the chicken is cooked through.

**4.** While the chicken cooks, add the broccoli rabe to the other sauté pan and season with salt and pepper. Cover and cook over high heat, stirring occasionally, until tender, about 4 minutes. Arrange the broccoli rabe on four plates, place the chicken on top. Serve.

# PRETZELIZED CHICKEN WITH CHEDDAR HORSERADISH SAUCE

**Number of Servings: 4**  *Estimated Cost: $16.25*

⅔ *cup canola oil*
**3 cups mini pretzels**
**3 eggs**
**4 thin-cut chicken cutlets (about 1¼ pounds total)**
*Salt and freshly ground black pepper*
**1 (8-ounce) tub horseradish cheddar cheese spread**
¼ *cup water*
**1 pound baby spinach**

**1.** Reserve 1 tablespoon of the oil. Heat the remaining oil in a very large sauté pan.

**2.** In a food processor, pulse the pretzels to fine crumbs, or crush with a rolling pin. Beat the eggs in a shallow bowl.

**3.** Season the chicken cutlets with salt and pepper. Dip into the eggs to coat, then dredge in the pretzel crumbs, pressing the crumbs onto the chicken. Add the chicken to the hot oil and cook for about 1½ minutes per side, or until golden brown, crispy, and cooked through.

**4.** Heat the cheese and water, covered with plastic wrap, in a microwave for about 3 minutes, stirring once until smooth, or in a small saucepan, stirring until smooth. Keep warm.

**5.** Remove the chicken from the pan and drain. Wipe the pan, set over high heat, and add the reserved oil. Add the spinach, season with salt and pepper, and stir. Cover and cook until wilted, about 1½ minutes, stirring occasionally. Serve the chicken on a bed of the spinach, spooning the cheese sauce over the top.

# MISO-WALNUT CHICKEN WITH RAINBOW SWISS CHARD

**Number of Servings: 4**  *Estimated Cost: $14*

½ cup corn oil
**½ cup miso paste**
**½ cup orange marmalade**
**½ cup chopped walnuts**
**4 thin chicken cutlets (about 1½ pounds total)**
**1 (16-ounce) package rainbow chard**
*Salt and freshly ground black pepper*

**1.** Heat ¼ cup of the oil in each of two large sauté pans until hot but not smoking.

**2.** Meanwhile, mix together the miso, marmalade, and walnuts. Lay the chicken on a work surface and spread the walnut mixture evenly over the top of each cutlet. Add 2 chicken cutlets to each pan, glaze side down, and cook until the glaze is charred. Turn and continue to cook until chicken is cooked through, approximately 3 more minutes.

**3.** Transfer the chicken to a plate and keep warm. Divide the chard between the hot pans. Season with salt and pepper, cover, and cook, stirring often, for 2 minutes, or until tender.

**4.** Arrange a bed of the chard on each plate and top with the chicken. Serve immediately.

# TURKEY CHOPPED STEAK WITH PEAS AND PICKLED ONIONS

**Number of Servings: 4**  *Estimated Cost: $13*

1¼ **pounds ground turkey**
*Salt and freshly ground black pepper*
**1 (15-ounce) jar Alfredo sauce**
½ **cup drained cocktail onions**
**1 cup frozen peas**
**1 (10-ounce) jar marinated whole mushrooms, drained and sliced in half**

**1.** Preheat a grill pan until very hot.

**2.** Meanwhile, season the turkey well with salt and pepper and form into 4 oval-shaped patties about ⅔ inch thick. Season the patties again with salt and pepper if necessary. Coat each patty lightly with cooking spray to prevent sticking.

**3.** Grill the turkey patties for 2½ minutes per side, or until just cooked through.

**4.** Meanwhile, heat the Alfredo sauce in a large sauté pan over medium heat. When the sauce begins to simmer, add the cocktail onions, peas, and mushrooms. Continue to simmer until all the vegetables are hot.

**5.** To serve, arrange the turkey patties on plates and spoon the sauce and vegetables over.

# TANGY TURKEY AND SNOW PEA STIR-FRY

**Number of Servings: 4**  *Estimated Cost: $18.75*

*2 cups water*
**2½ cups instant rice**
*3 tablespoons canola oil*
**1 pound turkey cutlets, cut into thin strips**
**1 (7-ounce) package raw sliced peppers and onions**
*Salt and freshly ground black pepper*
**4 ounces snow peas**
**1 (15-ounce) jar Patak's Tangy Lemon & Cilantro Cooking Sauce**
**(or other comparable sauce)**

**1.** Bring the water to a boil in a medium pot; season lightly with salt. Stir in the rice, cover, and turn off the heat. Allow the rice to stand for 5 minutes.

**2.** Meanwhile, heat the canola oil in a heavy 14-inch skillet until smoking. Add the turkey cutlet strips and stir-fry for 1 minute. Add the peppers and onions, season with salt and pepper, and stir-fry for 2 minutes. Add the snow peas and cook until they are tender, about 1 minute. Add the sauce and stir thoroughly to combine. Season with salt and pepper if necessary.

**3.** Make a bed of rice in the center of each of four plates and spoon the turkey mixture over the rice. Serve hot.

# TURKEY CUTLETS WITH RED KIDNEY BEANS, GARLIC RELISH, AND WATERCRESS

**Number of Servings: 4**  *Estimated Cost: $12*

*2 tablespoons canola oil*
**1½ pounds turkey breast cutlets, cut crosswise in half**
*Salt and freshly ground black pepper*
**3 (15-ounce) cans red kidney beans, drained, liquid reserved from 1½ cans**
**¼ cup prepared garlic relish**
**1 bunch watercress, trimmed and washed**

**1.** Heat the canola oil in a large sauté pan. Season the turkey with salt and pepper, add to the pan, and sauté until golden brown and just cooked through, about 2 minutes per side.

**2.** Meanwhile, in a separate large sauté pan, combine the beans, their reserved liquid, and the garlic relish and bring to a simmer. Mash the beans with a potato masher until almost smooth, leaving some chunks for texture. Season with salt and pepper.

**3.** To serve, spoon one-quarter of the bean mixture into each of four large bowls. Top with the turkey cutlets and serve with a pile of watercress on top of each.

# TURKEY, BROCCOLI, AND CHEESE CASSEROLE

**Number of Servings: 4**  *Estimated Cost: $19.75*

8 ounces frozen broccoli pieces
1 large commercially roasted turkey breast (about 2½ pounds),
skin removed and meat shredded (about 6 cups)
3 (10-ounce) cans cheddar cheese soup
*Salt and freshly ground black pepper*
1 (6-ounce) package Stovetop Turkey Stuffing Mix (or similar stuffing mix)
*2 tablespoons butter, melted*
*2 tablespoons water*

**1.** Bring a large pot of salted water to a boil. Cook the broccoli in the boiling water for about 30 seconds. Drain.

**2.** Mix the broccoli, turkey, and cheddar soup thoroughly in a large bowl. Season with salt and pepper. Spread the mixture evenly in a 13 x 9-inch casserole dish.

**3.** In a small bowl, mix together the stuffing mix, butter, and water. Cover the turkey mixture evenly with the stuffing mixture. Microwave for 3 to 3½ minutes, or until hot.

**4.** Meanwhile, preheat the broiler. Place the casserole under the broiler for 30 seconds to 1 minute, or until the stuffing turns golden brown. Serve hot.

# DUCK AND EGGPLANT FLASH-FRY

**Number of Servings: 4**  *Estimated Cost: $19.75*

*2 quarts corn oil*
*Flour for dredging*
*Salt and freshly ground black pepper*
**4 eggs**
**1 duck (about 6 pounds), skin removed, meat cut into 1-inch chunks**
**2 large eggplants, peeled and cut into 1-inch chunks (about 4 cups)**
**1¼ cups Thai peanut sauce**
**⅓ cup chopped fresh basil**

**1.** Heat the oil in a large pot until very hot but not smoking, about 400 degrees.

**2.** Meanwhile, spread the flour on a plate and season with salt and pepper. Beat the eggs in a shallow bowl.

**3.** Dredge the duck and eggplant in the flour, then dip in the eggs to coat. Add the duck and eggplant to the oil, being careful to separate any pieces that clump together. Fry for about 5 minutes. Drain on paper towels and season with salt and pepper.

**4.** In a large bowl, toss the fried duck and eggplant with the peanut sauce and basil. Serve immediately.

# Beef, Pork, and Lamb Main Dishes

# SIRLOIN TIPS WITH GORGONZOLA MASHED POTATOES

**Number of Servings: 4**  *Estimated Cost: $20*

1¼ cups heavy cream
1½ pounds store-bought precooked cubed golden potatoes
*2 tablespoons corn oil*
4 (6-ounce) sirloin tip steaks
*Salt and freshly ground black pepper*
1 cup frozen peas
1½ cups crumbled Gorgonzola cheese

**1.** Set two large sauté pans over high heat. Add the cream to one pan and bring to a boil. Add the potatoes to the cream and simmer until hot.

**2.** While the potatoes simmer, add the oil to the other pan and heat until hot. Season the steaks well with salt and pepper, add to the pan, and cook for about 2½ minutes per side (for rare), or to the desired doneness. Remove to a platter.

**3.** Microwave the peas, covered, for 2 to 3 minutes, or until hot; or cook on the stovetop according to the directions on the package. Set aside.

**4.** When the potatoes are hot, add the Gorgonzola and mash the mixture roughly with a potato masher or the back of a fork. Season with salt and pepper. Stir in the peas.

**5.** Mound the potatoes in the center of each plate. Lay the steaks against the potatoes.

# BROILED FLAT-IRON STEAKS WITH PEPPER JACK SCALLOPED POTATOES

**Number of Servings: 4** *Estimated Cost: $18.75*

1½ pounds store-bought precooked scallop-cut potatoes
½ cup heavy cream
*Salt and freshly ground black pepper*
8 ounces pepper Jack cheese, grated
4 (6- to 7-ounce) pieces flat-iron or sirloin steak, approximately 1 inch thick
½ cup A-1 Steak Sauce

**1.** Preheat the broiler. Spread the potatoes in a 13 x 17-inch baking dish. Drizzle the cream over the potatoes and season well with salt and pepper. Scatter the cheese evenly on top. Microwave on high for 4 minutes.

**2.** Meanwhile, season the steaks well with salt and pepper. Place on the broiling rack and broil for 2½ minutes per side, or until the desired doneness. Remove to a platter and allow to rest for a few minutes.

**3.** Place the potato dish under the broiler for 1 minute, or until the cheese is golden brown and bubbling.

**4.** Serve the potatoes alongside the steaks with the A-1 sauce.

# GRILLED FLANK STEAK WITH SHREDDED CARROTS AND PICKLED GINGER

**Number of Servings: 4**  *Estimated Cost: $19.50*

1¾ to 2 pounds sirloin steak, no more than ½ inch thick, cut into 4 equal portions
½ cup prepared garlic stir-fry and rib sauce
*Salt and freshly ground black pepper*
*2 tablespoons canola oil*
1 (8-ounce) package shredded carrots
⅓ cup drained pickled ginger, sliced
⅓ cup chopped fresh cilantro

**1.** Heat a grill pan until very hot.

**2.** Brush the steaks with about 2 tablespoons of the rib sauce, or just enough to coat. Season with salt and pepper. Grill for 2½ minutes per side for medium, or until cooked to the desired doneness.

**3.** Meanwhile, heat the oil in a large sauté pan until very hot. Add the carrots, stirring constantly for 2 to 3 minutes, or until they start to become tender. Add the pickled ginger and the remaining rib sauce and stir. Season with salt and pepper if necessary.

**4.** Slice the steaks in slices against the grain, if desired. Make a bed of the carrot-ginger mixture on each plate. Arrange the steaks on top, and sprinkle all with the cilantro.

# BEEF AND BROCCOLI-COLESLAW STIR-FRY

**Number of Servings: 4** *Estimated Cost: $16*

1½ cups water
**2 cups instant rice**
¼ cup canola oil
**1 (12-ounce) package broccoli coleslaw**
**1½ pounds boneless beef round, cut into ½-inch-wide strips**
*Salt and freshly ground black pepper*
**1½ cups prepared stir-fry sauce**
**⅓ cup chopped fresh basil**

**1.** In a medium saucepan, bring the water to a boil; season with salt. Add the rice, stir, cover tightly, and turn off the heat. Allow the rice to stand for 5 minutes.

**2.** Meanwhile, heat 2 tablespoons of the oil in a very large sauté pan until smoking. Add the broccoli coleslaw and stir-fry until the broccoli is somewhat tender, about 2 minutes. Remove the broccoli to a bowl; return the pan to the heat.

**3.** Season the beef lightly with salt and pepper. Add the beef to the hot pan and cook for about 1 minute, or until it has changed color; the meat will be rare. Add the stir-fry sauce and broccoli coleslaw and toss to coat the beef with sauce.

**4.** Fluff the cooked rice, and transfer to a platter or individual plates. Arrange the beef and broccoli mixture over the rice, and sprinkle the basil on top.

# BEEF AND ONION FLASH-FRY

**Number of Servings: 4**  *Estimated Cost: $16.25*

*2 quarts corn oil*
*Flour for dredging*
*Salt and freshly ground black pepper*
**4 eggs**
**3 large Vidalia onions, cut into ½-inch rings**
**1¼ to 1½ pounds boneless rib-eye steak, cut into 1-inch chunks**
**1¼ cups prepared sesame teriyaki sauce**
**⅓ cup chopped fresh cilantro**

**1.** Heat the oil in a large pot until almost smoking, about 400 degrees.

**2.** Meanwhile, spread the flour on a plate and season with salt and pepper. Beat the eggs in a shallow bowl.

**3.** Separate the onion rings. Dredge the beef and onions in the flour and dip into the eggs to coat. Carefully place the beef and onions in the hot oil, being sure to separate any pieces that stick together. Cook, stirring occasionally, for about 5 minutes, or until the beef is the desired doneness. Drain on paper towels and season with salt and pepper.

**4.** Place the beef and onions in a large bowl and toss with the sauce and cilantro. Serve hot.

# QUICK STEAK, PIZZA MAN STYLE

**Number of Servings: 4** *Estimated Cost: $20*

*3 tablespoons corn oil*
**4 (7-ounce) beef round sandwich steaks**
*Salt and freshly ground black pepper*
**1 (10.5-ounce) package diced green, red, and yellow bell peppers**
**⅔ cup dry red wine**
**⅔ cup beef broth**
**2½ cups prepared hot dog onions**

**1.** Heat 2 tablespoons of the oil in a very large sauté pan until smoking. Season the steaks with salt and pepper. Add to the pan and cook for about 2 minutes on each side for rare. Remove to a platter and let rest.

**2.** Meanwhile, heat the remaining tablespoon of oil in another large sauté pan. Add the peppers and cook, stirring frequently, for 1 minute. Add the red wine and simmer for about 1 minute, or until the liquid reduces and becomes syrupy.

**3.** Add the beef broth and onions and simmer for 1 minute more. Season with salt and pepper if necessary. Spoon on top of the steaks, and serve.

# BEEF CURRY SAUTÉ

**Number of Servings: 4**  *Estimated Cost: $19*

*1½ cups water*
**2 cups instant rice**
*1 tablespoon vegetable oil*
**1 cup diced green, red, and yellow bell peppers**
**2 tablespoons Patak's Hot Curry Paste (tomato and cumin)**
**1 (14-ounce) can coconut milk**
**1¼ pounds thickly sliced deli roast beef**
*Salt and freshly ground black pepper*

**1.** In a medium pot, bring the water to a boil; salt lightly. Stir in the rice, cover tightly, and turn off the heat. Allow the rice to stand for 5 minutes.

**2.** Meanwhile, heat the oil in a large sauté pan until hot. Add the diced peppers and cook, stirring frequently, until aromatic, about 1 minute. Add the curry paste and stir to mix. Stir in the coconut milk and bring the mixture to a simmer. Continue to simmer until the sauce begins to thicken.

**3.** Add the roast beef to the sauce. Season with salt and pepper and heat through. Remove from the heat.

**4.** Fluff the rice and divide it among four plates. Spoon the beef curry mixture over the rice, and serve.

# ROAST BEEF AND EGGPLANT ALFREDO

**Number of Servings: 4**  *Estimated Cost: $18.50*

*2 cups canola oil*
**2 cups prepared Alfredo sauce**
**2 large eggplants**
**1 pound sliced deli roast beef**
*Flour for dredging*
*Salt and freshly ground black pepper*
**3 eggs**
**3 cups bread crumbs**

**1.** Heat 1 cup of the oil in each of two large sauté pans until very hot.

**2.** Microwave the Alfredo sauce in a bowl for 3 minutes, or until very hot, stirring once. Or, heat it in a small saucepan over medium-high heat. Keep warm.

**3.** Trim each eggplant to about 5 inches long and 3 inches wide. Slice lengthwise into ⅜-inch-thick slices. You will need 8 slices total. Spread the flour on a plate and season with salt and pepper. Beat the eggs in a shallow bowl. Spread the bread crumbs on another plate.

**4.** Arrange 4 eggplant slices on a work surface and place one-quarter of the roast beef on top of each one. Top with the remaining 4 slices and press down firmly.

**5.** Dredge the stacks in the flour, dip into the eggs to coat, and then dredge in the bread crumbs to coat. Season well with salt and pepper. Place two stacks in each pan and sauté for 2½ minutes per side, or until golden brown and crispy. Drain on paper towels, then transfer to plates. Spoon about ½ cup hot Alfredo sauce on each eggplant stack, and serve.

# CHEESY ROAST BEEF AND ZUCCHINI

**Number of Servings: 4**  *Estimated Cost: $16*

*2 tablespoons canola oil*
**4 cups (¼ inch) zucchini slices, cut into half-moons**
*Salt and freshly ground black pepper*
**1 (15-ounce) jar salsa con queso**
**1 pound thinly sliced deli roast beef**

**1.** Heat a large sauté pan until hot. Add the oil and zucchini. Season the zucchini with salt and pepper and sauté, stirring frequently, until tender, about 5 minutes.

**2.** Meanwhile, pour the cheese sauce in a bowl and microwave until very hot. Alternatively, heat in a small saucepan over medium-high heat until hot.

**3.** Divide the zucchini among four plates and pile the roast beef on top. Spoon the hot cheese sauce liberally over the zucchini and beef. Serve.

# ROAST BEEF, CHESTNUTS, AND BRUSSELS SPROUTS IN CONSOMMÉ

**Number of Servings: 4**  *Estimated Cost: $17.75*

*1 tablespoon corn oil*
**1 (1 pint) small package Brussels sprouts, sliced thinly (about 4 cups)**
*Salt and freshly ground black pepper*
**1 pound thinly sliced deli roast beef, cut into 1-inch-wide strips**
**1 (7-ounce) jar chestnuts, sliced**
**2¼ cups beef broth**
**Grated zest of 3 lemons plus 1 teaspoon fresh lemon juice**

**1.** Heat the corn oil in a large sauté pan over high heat. Add the Brussels sprouts, season with salt and pepper, and stir-fry for about 2 minutes.

**2.** Meanwhile, arrange the beef on a plate and microwave until just hot, 2 to 3 minutes. Set aside.

**3.** Add the chestnuts and beef broth to the Brussels sprouts and bring to a simmer. Add the lemon zest and juice. Taste and season if necessary.

**4.** Divide the Brussels sprouts mixture among four bowls. Scatter the warm roast beef on top, and serve.

# BEEFY SHEPHERD'S PIE

**Number of Servings: 4** *Estimated Cost: $13.75*

**4 cups prepared garlic mashed potatoes**
*1 tablespoon corn oil*
**1½ pounds ground beef**
**1 cup frozen peas**
**1 (12-ounce) jar home-style beef gravy**
*Salt and freshly ground black pepper*
**1 (8-ounce) package shredded sharp cheddar cheese**

**1.** Preheat the broiler. Microwave the mashed potatoes until hot, about 4 minutes; stir occasionally.

**2.** Meanwhile, heat the oil in a large sauté pan until very hot. Add the ground beef and cook, stirring to break up the meat, for 3 minutes. Add the peas and gravy and bring to a simmer.

**3.** Spread the beef mixture in a 12 x 7½-inch baking dish. Spread the mashed potatoes evenly over the beef, covering it completely. Sprinkle the cheese over the potatoes. Place under the broiler until the cheese melts, about 1 minute. Serve hot.

# GROUND BEEF WITH REFRIED BEANS, SALSA, AND GRILLED ZUCCHINI

**Number of Servings: 4** *Estimated Cost: $10.50*

**3 zucchini, cut lengthwise into ⅓-inch-thick strips**
*5 tablespoons corn oil*
*Salt and freshly ground black pepper*
**1½ pounds ground beef, preferably 80% lean**
**1 (16-ounce) can refried beans**
*½ cup water*
**1 (14-ounce) container fresh salsa**
**4 large taco shells**

**1.** Heat a grill pan and a large sauté pan until very hot.

**2.** Toss the zucchini with 3 tablespoons of the oil and season well with salt and pepper. Grill the zucchini, turning once, for 5 minutes, or until tender.

**3.** Meanwhile, add the remaining 2 tablespoons oil to the sauté pan. Add the beef, season with salt and pepper, and cook, stirring, until the beef is almost cooked through.

**4.** Combine the refried beans, water, and salsa in a bowl, stirring to combine. Add to the beef mixture and simmer until the beef is cooked through.

**5.** To serve, place the zucchini strips in the bottoms of the tortilla shells. Spoon the beef mixture on top of the zucchini, and serve immediately.

# GROUND BEEF WITH SALSA VERDE, RADICCHIO, AND SOUR CREAM

**Number of Servings: 4**  *Estimated Cost: $12.75*

*1 tablespoon corn oil*
**1½ pounds ground beef**
*Salt and freshly ground black pepper*
**1 (16-ounce) can refried beans**
*½ cup water*
**1 cup prepared green salsa (salsa verde)**
**3 cups shredded radicchio (about 1 medium head)**
**½ cup sour cream**

**1.** Heat the oil in a very large sauté pan until very hot. Add the ground beef and stir to break up the meat. Season with salt and pepper.

**2.** Whisk together the refried beans and water in a medium bowl. Add the mixture to the beef, stir, and simmer until the beef is completely cooked through. Stir in the salsa verde.

**3.** Divide half of the radicchio among four large bowls. Spoon the beef mixture on top. Top with the sour cream and the remaining radicchio. Serve.

# CORNED BEEF BRISKET WITH CABBAGE, POTATOES, AND HORSERADISH

**Number of Servings: 4**  *Estimated Cost: $16.50*

*1 tablespoon canola oil*
**3 cups coleslaw mix**
**2 cups store-bought precooked scallop-cut potatoes**
*Salt and freshly ground black pepper*
**1½ (14-ounce) cans beef broth**
**½ cup prepared horseradish**
**1 pound sliced corned beef brisket**

**1.** Heat the oil in a very large sauté pan. Add the coleslaw mix and sauté for 1 minute. Add the potatoes and sauté for another minute. Season with salt and pepper.

**2.** Add the beef broth and bring to a boil. Stir in the horseradish. Lay the slices of beef brisket across the vegetables. Cover and cook at a very low simmer for about 2 minutes, or until the beef is heated through.

**3.** Ladle the beef mixture into hot bowls and serve.

# VEAL SCALOPPINI IN ARTICHOKE BROTH

**Number of Servings: 4** *Estimated Cost: $18.75*

*2 tablespoons canola oil*
**1¼ pounds veal scaloppini**
*Salt and freshly ground black pepper*
**4 cups prepared country-style mashed potatoes**
*3 tablespoons extra virgin olive oil*
**3 large cloves garlic, chopped**
**1½ tablespoons fresh thyme leaves**
**1½ (14-ounce) cans quartered artichoke hearts, drained, 1¼ cups liquid reserved**

**1.** Heat the canola oil in a large sauté pan over medium-low heat. Season the veal lightly with salt and pepper and sauté, turning once, just until cooked through.

**2.** Meanwhile, microwave the mashed potatoes for about 5 minutes, stirring twice.

**3.** While the veal is cooking, heat the olive oil in another large sauté pan until hot. Add the garlic and thyme and sauté until the garlic is fragrant but not brown. Add the reserved 1¼ cups artichoke liquid along with the artichoke hearts and bring to a boil. Simmer until the artichoke hearts are hot. Season with salt and pepper if necessary.

**4.** To serve, place a mound of the potatoes in the center of each plate. Spoon the broth and artichokes around the potatoes and top with the veal scaloppini. Serve hot.

# 12 EGGS IN A PAN

**Number of Servings: 4**  *Estimated Cost: $7.25*

*3 tablespoons olive oil*
**2 cups zucchini slices, cut into half-moons**
**3 cooked hot Italian sausages, sliced**
**3 cloves garlic, chopped**
*Salt and freshly ground black pepper*
**12 eggs, cracked into a bowl but yolks not broken**
**1 (8-ounce) package shredded mozzarella/provolone blend**

**1.** Preheat the broiler. Heat the olive oil in a large cast-iron skillet until hot but not smoking. Add the zucchini and sausage to the pan and cook for 1½ minutes. Add the garlic and cook for another 30 seconds, stirring frequently. Season with salt and pepper.

**2.** Gently pour the eggs into the pan, being careful not to break the yolks. Place the pan under the broiler and cook for 1½ minutes. Sprinkle the cheese evenly over the top and broil for another minute, or until the cheese is melted and the whites of the eggs are set. Serve immediately.

# ANDOUILLE SAUSAGE JAMBALAYA WITH CLAMS AND PEAS

**Number of Servings: 4** *Estimated Cost: $13.50*

*1 tablespoon corn oil*
**12 ounces cooked andouille sausage, cut into 1-inch pieces**
**1½ cups frozen peas**
**3 (6.5-ounce) cans chopped clams, drained, liquid reserved**
**3 cups instant rice**
**1 (12-ounce) jar Goya Sofrito**
*Salt and freshly ground black pepper*

**1.** Heat the corn oil in a large sauté pan until hot but not smoking. Add the andouille and cook until the sausage begins to color and is hot throughout, about 4 minutes. Add the peas and clams and cook until just heated through.

**2.** While the sausage is cooking, add enough water to the clam liquid to total 2½ cups. Bring to a boil in a medium pot. Add the rice, stir, and turn off heat. Cover and allow the rice to stand for 5 minutes.

**3.** Add the sofrito to the sausage and peas and stir. Fluff the rice, add to the pan, and season with salt and pepper if necessary. Serve hot.

# BARBECUE KIELBASA WITH CORN, BLACK BEANS, AND CORN MUFFINS

**Number of Servings: 4**  *Estimated Cost: $12*

*2 tablespoons corn oil*
**1¼ pounds kielbasa, halved lengthwise and cut into 1-inch half-moons**
**2 (14-ounce) cans black beans, drained**
**1 (10-ounce) package frozen succotash**
**1¾ cups barbecue sauce**
*½ cup water*
**4 corn muffin tops**

**1.** Heat the oil in a Dutch oven or other large pot until hot. Add the kielbasa and cook, stirring, until browned. Add the beans, succotash, barbecue sauce, and water. Bring to a simmer and simmer until heated through.

**2.** Place 1 corn muffin top in each of four bowls. Ladle the stew into the bowls, and serve.

# CHORIZO AND MANCHEGO FRITTATA WITH MESCLUN SALAD

**Number of Servings: 4**  *Estimated Cost: $20*

*1 tablespoon canola oil*
**8 ounces Spanish-style chorizo, halved lengthwise and cut into ¼-inch slices**
**14 eggs**
**2 cups grated Manchego cheese**
*Salt and freshly ground black pepper*
**1 (7-ounce) package mesclun salad mix**
*1 tablespoon sherry vinegar*
*2 tablespoons extra virgin olive oil*

**1.** Preheat the oven to 500 degrees.

**2.** Heat the canola oil in a 12-inch sauté pan. Add the chorizo and sauté for 45 seconds or until hot. Beat the eggs in a large bowl, add half the cheese, and season with salt and pepper. Add the eggs to the pan and stir until large curds form but the eggs are still wet.

**3.** Sprinkle the remaining cheese on top of the frittata and place in the oven. Bake for about 2 minutes, or until the cheese is melted and the eggs are just set. Remove from the oven and loosen the sides of the frittata with a spatula. Invert onto a cutting board.

**4.** Meanwhile, mix the sherry vinegar and olive oil. Toss the mesclun with this dressing and season with salt and pepper.

**5.** Cut the frittata into 8 wedges, placing 2 on each plate, and serve with a pile of salad.

# HOT ITALIAN SAUSAGE WITH FRESH BEANS AND BEETS

**Number of Servings: 4**  *Estimated Cost: $15*

4 tablespoons extra virgin olive oil
**2 (14-ounce) jars Harvard beets, drained, liquid reserved**
**8 ounces green beans, trimmed and cut in half**
**8 ounces wax beans, trimmed and cut in half**
*Salt and freshly ground black pepper*
**8 cooked hot Italian sausages, cut into 1-inch slices**
**3 tablespoons chopped fresh chives**

**1.** Heat 2 tablespoons of the oil in a large sauté pan.

**2.** Microwave the beets, covered, for 3 to 4 minutes, or until very hot.

**3.** Meanwhile, add the beans to the hot pan and cook, stirring often, for about 1 minute. Season with salt and pepper. Add the sausage and cook for another 2 minutes, or until the beans are tender and the sausage is hot throughout.

**4.** Mix the reserved beet liquid with the chives in a bowl. Float the remaining 2 tablespoons of oil on top.

**5.** Divide the beets among four plates. Top with the sausage-bean mixture. Spoon the beet sauce over the top, and serve.

# CHORIZO, SMOKED MUSSEL, AND OKRA RICE PILAF

**Number of Servings: 4**  *Estimated Cost: $12.50*

**1½ cups frozen sliced okra, thawed**
*3 tablespoons sherry vinegar*
**2½ cups water**
**3 cups instant rice**
*1 tablespoon canola oil*
**12 ounces Spanish-style chorizo, halved lengthwise and cut into 1-inch slices**
*Salt and freshly ground black pepper*
**1 (3.5-ounce) can smoked mussels**
**1 cup Goya Recaito**

**1.** Combine the okra with the vinegar in a bowl. Set aside to marinate.

**2.** In a medium pot, bring the water to a boil; season with salt. Add the rice, stir, cover, and turn off the heat. Allow the rice to stand for 5 minutes.

**3.** Meanwhile, heat the oil in a large sauté pan. Add the chorizo and sauté for 1 minute. Add the okra and vinegar and cook for 3 minutes, stirring occasionally. Season with salt and pepper.

**4.** Add the mussels and recaito seasoning and cook until hot. Fluff the rice and toss with the mussel mixture. Season with salt and pepper if necessary.

**5.** Transfer the pilaf to plates and serve hot.

# KIELBASA AND SAUERKRAUT STEW

**Number of Servings: 4** *Estimated Cost: $10.25*

*2 tablespoons corn oil*
**1¾ pounds kielbasa, cut into ¾ inch slices**
**1½ pounds prepared sauerkraut**
*Salt and freshly ground black pepper*
**½ cup Dijon mustard**

**1.** Heat the oil in a large sauté pan until hot. Add the kielbasa slices and cook until browned on the first side, about 2 minutes. Turn and add the sauerkraut. Cover and cook for another 3 minutes, or until heated through. Season with salt and pepper if necessary.

**2.** Serve the stew with the mustard on the side.

# BONELESS PORK CHOPS WITH POTATO PANCAKES AND MUSTARD GREENS

**Number of Servings: 4**  *Estimated Cost: $15*

**1 (12-ounce) jar apple jelly**
**5 tablespoons Dijon mustard**
*¼ cup plus 3 tablespoons canola oil*
**1½ pounds thin-cut boneless pork chops**
*Salt and freshly ground black pepper*
**4 prepared potato pancakes**
**1½ bunches mustard greens, washed and cut into large pieces**

**1.** Put the apple jelly in a large bowl and microwave for 5 minutes; it will reduce slightly. Whisk in the mustard and set aside.

**2.** Meanwhile, pour 3 tablespoons of the oil into one large sauté pan and the remaining ¼ cup oil into another large sauté pan. Heat until hot. Season the chops with salt and pepper and add to the first pan. Cook, turning once, until golden brown on both sides and just cooked through, about 5 minutes.

**3.** While the pork is cooking, cook the pancakes over medium-high heat in the other pan, for about 1½ minutes per side, or until they are crispy and heated through. Drain on paper towels and season with salt and pepper.

**4.** Add the mustard greens to the oil remaining in the potato pancake pan and sauté until wilted, about 2 minutes. Season with salt and pepper.

**5.** Arrange a chop, a pancake, and a pile of mustard greens on each plate. Spoon apple jelly sauce over all. Serve.

# PORK SCALOPPINI STUFFED WITH CHEDDAR

**Number of Servings: 4**  *Estimated Cost: $13.25*

*1 cup plus 2 tablespoons canola oil*
**4 cups Cheez-It or other cheddar crackers**
*Flour for dredging*
*Salt and freshly ground black pepper*
**4 eggs**
**8 thin slices pork cutlet, sliced (1¼ pounds total)**
**8 ounces sharp cheddar, cut into 8 slices**
**1 (12-ounce) package broccoli coleslaw**

**1.** Heat ½ cup of the oil in each of two large sauté pans until hot.

**2.** Meanwhile, in the bowl of a food processor, pulse half of the Cheez-It crackers to coarse crumbs; transfer to a shallow bowl. Repeat with the remaining Cheez-It crackers. Spread the flour on a plate and season with salt and pepper. Beat the eggs in a shallow dish.

**3.** Lay 4 cutlets on a work surface. Put 2 cheddar slices, side by side, on each cutlet so that it is almost completely covered. Top each with another cutlet and press with your hands so the meat sticks together.

**4.** Dredge each pork stack in the flour, dip in eggs to coat, and dredge in the Cheez-It crumbs, turning to coat evenly. Place 2 pork cutlet stacks in each pan and cook until golden brown on both sides, about 1½ minutes per side. Remove and drain on paper towels.

**5.** Wipe each pan and add 1 tablespoon of the remaining oil. Add half of the broccoli coleslaw to each pan and sauté, stirring often, for about 2 minutes, or until tender but not mushy. Season with salt and pepper and divide among 4 plates. Serve the scaloppini on top.

# PORK AND ZUCCHINI FLASH-FRY WITH BLACK BEAN SAUCE

**Number of Servings: 4**  *Estimated Cost: $12.75*

*2 quarts corn oil*
*Flour for dredging*
*Salt and freshly ground black pepper*
**4 eggs**
**1¼ pounds boneless pork loin, cut into 1-inch strips**
**2 medium zucchini, cut into 1-inch chunks**
**1¼ cups Chinese black bean sauce**
**¼ cup roughly chopped fresh mint**

**1.** Heat the oil in a large pot until very hot but not smoking, about 400 degrees.

**2.** Meanwhile, spread the flour on a plate and season with salt and pepper. Beat the eggs in a shallow bowl. Dredge the pork and zucchini in the flour, then toss with the eggs to coat.

**3.** Add the pork and zucchini to the pot, being careful to separate any pieces that have stuck together. Cook for about 5 minutes, stirring occasionally. Drain on paper towels and season with salt and pepper.

**4.** Transfer the pork and zucchini to a large bowl and toss with the sauce and mint. Serve immediately.

# SAUTÉED PORK WITH SNOW PEAS, WALNUTS, AND BEETS

**Number of Servings: 4**  *Estimated Cost: $16*

¼ cup olive oil
**4 thin-cut boneless pork chops (about 1½ pounds total)**
*Salt and freshly ground black pepper*
**⅔ cup crushed walnuts**
**8 ounces fresh snow peas**
**2 cups sliced pickled beets, drained**
**⅓ cup hot dog relish**

**1.** Heat 1 tablespoon of the oil in a large sauté pan over high heat. Season the pork with salt and pepper and place in the pan. Cook for about 1½ minutes per side, or until the desired doneness. Remove from the pan and set aside.

**2.** Add the remaining 3 tablespoons oil to the pan and heat until very hot. Add the walnuts and cook until fragrant, then add the snow peas and cook for about 30 seconds. Add the beets and relish and toss to coat the beets and snow peas. Continue to cook until the vegetable mixture is heated through. Season with salt and pepper.

**3.** Divide the vegetable mixture among four plates and place the pork alongside. Serve.

# STUFFED PORK CHOPS WITH BOURSIN AND COLLARDS

**Number of Servings: 4** *Estimated Cost: $19.75*

½ cup plus 2 tablespoons canola oil
Flour for dredging
Salt and freshly ground black pepper
**3 eggs**
**1½ cups dried bread crumbs**
**1 (5.2-ounce) package Boursin cheese, slightly softened**
**8 thin center-cut boneless pork loin chops (just under 1¼ pounds total)**
**12 ounces trimmed collard greens**

**1.** Pour ½ cup of the oil into one large sauté pan, pour the remaining 2 tablespoons into another large sauté pan, and heat until hot. (Turn down the heat under the second pan if the oil begins to smoke, then turn it up again before adding the greens.)

**2.** Meanwhile, spread the flour on a plate and season with salt and pepper. Beat the eggs in a shallow bowl. Spread the bread crumbs on another plate.

**3.** Spread one-quarter of the Boursin evenly on each of 4 of the pork chops. Top each with another pork chop and press down firmly. Dredge the chops in the flour, dip in the eggs, and then dredge in the bread crumbs. Place the chops in the pan with ½ cup oil. Cook until golden brown on the first side, about 2½ minutes. Flip the chops and cook for another 2½ minutes, or until cooked through.

**4.** Meanwhile, add the collard greens to the second pan and season with salt and pepper. Cook for 5 minutes, stirring constantly, until the greens are wilted and tender but not mushy. Remove the pork chops from the pan and drain. Serve each chop with a pile of collards alongside.

# GRILLED BONELESS LEG OF LAMB WITH GREEK YOGURT SAUCE

**Number of Servings: 4**  *Estimated Cost: $18.75*

*2 cups water*
**2½ cups instant rice**
**4 thin-cut boneless leg of lamb steaks (1¼ to 1½ pounds total), pounded ¾ inch thick if necessary**
*1 tablespoon corn oil*
*Salt and freshly ground black pepper*
**1 large seedless cucumber, halved lengthwise, then sliced crosswise into very thin half-moons**
**1 cup plain yogurt, preferably Greek**
**⅓ cup chopped fresh mint**

**1.** Heat a grill pan until very hot.

**2.** Meanwhile, bring the water to a boil in a medium pot over high heat; season with salt. Add the rice, stir, cover, and turn off the heat. Let the rice stand for 5 minutes.

**3.** Coat the lamb with the oil and season liberally with salt and pepper. Grill for about 2 minutes on each side. Remove to a plate and allow to rest.

**4.** Meanwhile, combine the cucumber, yogurt, and mint in a bowl. Season with salt and pepper.

**5.** Slice the lamb. Fluff the rice with a fork and spoon a pile onto each plate. Top with the cucumber salad and then the lamb. Serve.

# GRILLED LAMB WITH SWEET-AND-SOUR CRANBERRY SAUCE

**Number of Servings: 4** *Estimated Cost: $16*

**1 cup dried cranberries, chopped**
*½ cup water*
*¼ cup sugar*
*2 tablespoons white vinegar*
**2 tablespoons Dijon mustard**
*Salt and freshly ground black pepper*
**3 cloves garlic, chopped**
*¼ cup extra virgin olive oil*
**4 thin-cut boneless leg of lamb steaks (about 1½ pounds total), pounded ¾ inch thick if necessary**
**5 small zucchini, cut lengthwise into quarters**

**1.** Heat a grill pan until very hot.

**2.** Meanwhile, combine the cranberries, water, sugar, and vinegar in a small saucepan and bring to a boil. Reduce the heat and simmer slowly for 4 minutes, or until the cranberries are plump and the sauce is slightly thickened. Stir in the mustard and season with salt and pepper.

**3.** Combine the garlic and olive oil in a large bowl. Toss the lamb and zucchini in the mixture to coat. Season liberally with salt and pepper.

**4.** Grill the lamb, turning once, for 5 minutes, or until the desired doneness. Grill the zucchini alongside the lamb, turning often.

**5.** Serve the lamb and zucchini with the cranberry sauce.

# Desserts

# ANGEL FOOD AND CHERRY CAKE WITH GINGER CREAM

**Number of Servings: 4**  *Estimated Cost: $10.50*

**1 (8-inch) piece ginger, cut into 2-inch chunks**
*1 teaspoon sugar (if you don't have a juicer)*
**8 ounces cherry preserves**
**1 (15-ounce) can cherry pie filling, drained**
**1 cup very cold heavy cream**
*Pinch of salt*
**4 large slices angel food cake**

**1.** Juice the ginger with a juicer. Or, if you don't have a juicer, place the ginger and sugar in the bowl of a food processor and pulse until the ginger is chopped fine. Then wrap the ginger in a thin cloth and wring out all the juice into a bowl. Set aside.

**2.** In a small bowl, heat the cherry preserves in a microwave until liquefied, about 1 minute. Stir in the cherry pie filling.

**3.** Combine 3 tablespoons of the ginger juice with the cream in a medium bowl and add the salt. Whip the ginger cream until soft peaks form.

**4.** Lay the angel food cake slices on four plates. Top each slice with one-quarter of the cherry mixture, allowing the liquid to soak into the cake. Top each with a large dollop of the ginger whipped cream. Serve immediately.

# APRICOT AND DRIED CHERRY POUND CAKE

**Number of Servings: 4**  *Estimated Cost: $10.50*

1 (15-ounce) can apricot halves in light syrup, drained, liquid reserved
½ cup dried cherries
4 slices pound cake
1¼ cups peaches and cream ice cream
12 fresh basil leaves, slivered

**1.** In a small pot, bring the reserved apricot liquid and the cherries to a boil. Reduce the heat and simmer for 3 minutes.

**2.** Add the apricots to the pot, stir to combine, and heat through.

**3.** Lay a slice of pound cake on each of four plates. Top with the apricot-cherry mixture, letting the sauce soak into the cake. Place a large scoop of ice cream on top of each and scatter the basil over and around. Serve immediately.

# BLUEBERRY POMEGRANATE CONSOMMÉ WITH WHIPPED CRÈME FRAÎCHE

**Number of Servings: 4**  *Estimated Cost: $11.25*

**6 ounces crème fraîche**
*1 teaspoon sugar*
*Pinch of salt*
**36 blackberries**
**1½ cups mango sorbet**
**1 cup blueberry pomegranate juice**
**¼ cup crushed Froot Loops**

**1.** Whip the crème fraîche with the sugar and salt just until soft to medium peaks form; do not overwhip.

**2.** Make 3 clusters of 3 blackberries each in the bottom of four shallow bowls, spacing the clusters so that they represent the points of a triangle. Place a large scoop of mango sorbet in the center of each bowl. Pour ¼ cup of the juice into the bottom of each bowl. Place a small dollop of crème fraîche on top of each cluster of blackberries.

**3.** Sprinkle the Froot Loops evenly over the desserts and serve immediately.

# CARAMELIZED BANANA PANINI

**Number of Servings: 4**  *Estimated Cost: $6.75*

*⅓ cup sugar*
**4 slices challah bread**
**3 ripe bananas, peeled**
*Pinch of salt*
*8 to 12 tablespoons (1 to 1½ sticks) butter*
**¼ cup fresh lime juice**
**1 pint pineapple coconut ice cream**

**1.** Heat a large nonstick sauté pan over medium heat. Meanwhile, pour the sugar onto a plate. Coat the challah slices on both sides with sugar. Slice each banana crosswise in half, then slice each half lengthwise into 3 slices, giving you 18 slices. Arrange 4 banana slices across the top of each piece of bread and press slightly so that bananas stick to the bread. Season the bananas lightly with salt.

**2.** Add 1 stick butter to the hot pan. When the butter is melted, place all 4 panini in the pan, banana side down. Cook until caramelized, then flip each one over. Add up to 4 more tablespoons butter if the pan is dry. Cook for about 2 more minutes.

**3.** Sprinkle 2 tablespoons of the remaining sugar on the plate around the panini and add the lime juice to the pan. Simmer until the sugar dissolves and forms a sauce, then use the sauce to baste the panini.

**4.** Place the panini on individual plates. Top each one with a large scoop of pineapple coconut ice cream and serve immediately.

# CHOCOLATE PHYLLO WITH BLOOD ORANGES AND DULCE DE LECHE ICE CREAM

**Number of Servings: 4**  *Estimated Cost: $10.25*

*10 tablespoons (1¼ sticks) butter, melted*
**5 tablespoons unsweetened cocoa powder**
**8 sheets frozen phyllo, thawed**
*Sugar*
**1 pint dulce de leche or caramel ice cream**
**5 blood or navel oranges, peeled and separated into segments**

**1.** Preheat the oven to 425 degrees.

**2.** In a bowl, mix the melted butter and cocoa powder. Lay a sheet of phyllo on a work surface (cover the remaining sheets with a damp towel). Brush with the butter mixture, then sprinkle liberally with sugar. Cover with another sheet of phyllo; repeat until you have a stack of 4 layers; transfer to a parchment-lined baking sheet. Make another stack with the remaining phyllo; place on another parchment-lined baking sheet.

**3.** Bake the stacks for 5 minutes or until crispy. Allow to cool, then break into 8 pieces.

**4.** Lay 1 piece of phyllo on each plate and top with a scoop of ice cream. Scatter the oranges over and around the ice cream. Prop another piece of phyllo up against each scoop of the ice cream, and serve.

# COCOA COOKIES WITH BLACK RASPBERRY ICE CREAM AND CHOCOLATE FUDGE

**Number of Servings: 4**  *Estimated Cost: $12.25*

¾ **cup fudge sauce**
**8 soft chocolate cookies**
**1 pint black raspberry ice cream**
**8 ounces fresh blackberries**

**1.** Microwave the fudge sauce in a small bowl for about 1 minute, until hot; stir halfway through cooking.

**2.** Spread the cookies on a large plate and microwave them for 30 seconds.

**3.** Stack 2 cookies each in the center of four plates. Place a large scoop of the ice cream on top of each cookie pile. Pour fudge sauce on top of the ice cream and cookies and scatter the blackberries over and around. Serve immediately.

# DOUGHNUTS AND HOT CHOCOLATE

**Number of Servings: 4**  *Estimated Cost: $12.25*

**4 cups half-and-half**
*2 tablespoons sugar*
*½ teaspoon salt*
**6 ounces bittersweet chocolate, finely chopped**
**4 powdered sugar doughnuts**

**1.** In a medium pot, bring the half-and-half, sugar, and salt to a boil. Turn off the heat and add the chocolate. Allow to sit for 1 minute, then whisk until the chocolate is completely melted.

**2.** Pour the hot chocolate into four mugs and serve a doughnut with each mug.

# GRILLED PINEAPPLE WITH COCOA FOAM

**Number of Servings: 4**  *Estimated Cost: $5.25*

**1 large pineapple, cored and peeled**
*Salt*
**1 cup nonfat milk**
**¼ cup chocolate syrup**
**3 tablespoons cocoa powder**
*1 tablespoon sugar*

**1.** Preheat a grill pan until hot. Make sure the grill pan is very clean; brush the pan with oil.

**2.** Cut the pineapple crosswise into eight ½-inch-thick slices. Season very lightly with salt. Grill for 2½ minutes per side, or until they have grill marks on both sides and are hot throughout. Remove from the grill.

**3.** Meanwhile, heat the milk and chocolate syrup in a small pot until simmering. Whisk in the cocoa powder, sugar, and a large pinch of salt. Blend this mixture with a hand-held immersion blender until very frothy.

**4.** Place 2 pineapple rings on each plate. Using a large spoon, skim the foam from the top of the cocoa mixture and spoon the foam over the pineapples to cover them. You will need to refroth the foam after each skimming. Serve immediately.

# INSTANT TIRAMISU WITH RASPBERRIES

**Number of Servings: 4**  *Estimated Cost: $14.25*

¾ **cup mocha sauce**
**20 soft ladyfingers**
**1 pint coffee ice cream**
½ **pint fresh raspberries**

**1.** In a small bowl, heat the mocha sauce in the microwave for about 1 minute, or until hot; stir.

**2.** Lay 5 ladyfingers on each plate to form a pentagon. Place a large scoop of ice cream in the center of each pentagon and spoon some of the mocha sauce over and around it. Scatter raspberries on each plate, and serve immediately.

# CRISPY WONTON WAFERS WITH LEMON CURD AND STRAWBERRIES

**Number of Servings: 4**  *Estimated Cost: $11.50*


*2 quarts canola oil*
**13 wonton skins**
*Sugar*
**1⅓ cups very cold heavy cream**
**1¼ cups plus 2 tablespoons prepared lemon curd**
**12 strawberries, hulled and thinly sliced**
**1 cup lemon sorbet**


**1.** In a large pot, heat the oil to 325 degrees. Fry the wontons, 3 to 4 at a time, for about 1 minute, or until golden brown; use a mesh strainer to periodically flip them and keep them submerged to ensure even cooking. Drain on paper towels and sprinkle lightly with sugar. Set aside.

**2.** Whip the cream in a medium bowl until stiff peaks form.

**3.** To assemble, smear 1½ tablespoons of the curd onto the center of each of 12 wontons. Arrange the slices from 1 strawberry in the curd on each wonton. Place a large dollop of whipped cream on top of the strawberries. Place a small dollop of whipped cream on each plate. Place 1 wonton on top of the cream and shingle 2 more across the plate.

**4.** Crush the remaining wonton into small pieces and put a small pile next to each dessert. Place a small scoop of lemon sorbet on top of the crushed wonton and serve.

# PEARS IN PHYLLO CUPS WITH BUTTER PECAN ICE CREAM AND CARAMEL SAUCE

**Number of Servings: 4** *Estimated Cost: $9.25*

**8 sheets frozen phyllo, at room temperature**
*⅔ stick (approximately 5 tablespoons) butter, melted*
**1 (15-ounce) can pear halves in juice, drained**
*Salt*
**⅔ cup caramel sauce**
**1¼ cups butter pecan ice cream**

**1.** Preheat the oven to 450 degrees.

**2.** Lay a sheet of phyllo on a work surface (cover the remaining sheets with a damp towel) and brush with butter. Top with another sheet and brush with butter. Repeat the process until you have a stack of 4 sheets. Cut two 7-inch squares from this stack. Repeat with the remaining phyllo, so you have 4 phyllo squares.

**3.** Press each phyllo square into one of the cups of a Texas (jumbo) muffin pan, molding it into the shape of the cup; you will have some overhang. Bake for about 4½ minutes, or until golden and crispy. Remove the phyllo cups from the pan and set aside.

**4.** Meanwhile, thinly slice the pears and place on a plate. Season lightly with salt. Microwave for 1 minute, or until hot; set aside. Microwave the caramel sauce in a small bowl for 1½ minutes, or until hot.

**5.** Arrange the pear slices in the center of four plates. Place a phyllo cup on top of the pears and arrange the remaining pears inside the cups. Add a scoop of ice cream on top of each cup, and spoon warm caramel sauce over and around. Serve immediately.

# PRETTY PEACH MELBA

**Number of Servings: 4**  *Estimated Cost: $13.50*

**8 sheets frozen phyllo dough, at room temperature**
*8 tablespoons (1 stick) butter, melted*
*½ cup sugar*
**1 teaspoon ground cinnamon**
**4 large scoops vanilla ice cream, about 1 pint**
**4 large canned peach halves**
**¾ cup prepared raspberry sauce**

**1.** Preheat the oven to 450 degrees.

**2.** Lay a sheet of phyllo on a work surface (cover the remaining sheets with a damp towel) and brush with butter. Sprinkle with sugar and cinnamon. Cover with another sheet of phyllo, and repeat the process until you have a stack of 4 sheets. Lay on a parchment-lined baking sheet. Repeat with the remaining phyllo to make another 4-layer stack. Place on another parchment-lined baking sheet.

**3.** Bake the stacks for 5 minutes, or until golden brown and crispy. Allow to cool. Break off a very small piece of phyllo and crush it into crumbs. Place a small pile of the crumbs in the center of each of four bowls. Put a scoop of vanilla ice cream on top of the crumbs in each bowl. Top each scoop with a peach half (cut side down), and press it gently into the ice cream. Spoon the raspberry sauce over and around the peaches.

**4.** Break the remaining phyllo into large haphazard pieces; lay a piece across each peach, and serve.

# S'MORES TARTLETS

**Number of Servings: 4**  *Estimated Cost: $9.75*

**8 mini graham cracker piecrusts or tartlet shells**
**8 ounces bittersweet chocolate, finely chopped**
**8 large strawberries, hulled and sliced**
**1½ cups marshmallow creme**
*Salt*

**1.** Preheat a toaster oven to high or turn on the oven broiler. Bake the tart shells until golden brown, 1½ minutes. Remove from the toaster oven or broiler, and turn the toaster oven setting to dark toast.

**2.** Meanwhile, melt the chocolate in a double boiler over low heat.

**3.** Spoon a little more than a tablespoon of chocolate into the bottom of each tart shell and arrange the slices from 1 strawberry in the chocolate. Spoon about 3 tablespoons of marshmallow creme into each shell and spread it out to the edges of the shell. Sprinkle a tiny amount of salt on top of each.

**4.** Place the tartlets in the toaster oven or under the broiler. Watch carefully until the marshmallow creme becomes toasty brown. Remove from the oven.

**5.** Place 2 tartlets on each plate and drizzle the chocolate over them and the plates. Serve immediately.

# WARM RICE PUDDING WITH RUM RAISIN ICE CREAM

**Number of Servings: 4**  *Estimated Cost: $9.25*

**8 sheets frozen phyllo, thawed**
*⅔ stick (approximately 5 tablespoons) butter, melted*
*Sugar*
**1 (22-ounce) package prepared rice pudding**
**1½ cups rum raisin ice cream**

**1.** Preheat the oven to 450 degrees.

**2.** Lay a sheet of phyllo on a work surface (cover the remaining sheets with a damp towel). Brush it liberally with melted butter and sprinkle with a little sugar. Top with a second sheet, brush with butter, and sprinkle with sugar. Gently scrunch the phyllo up, forming a rough circle about 7 inches in diameter. Place it on a parchment-lined sheet. Repeat the process with the remaining phyllo, making a total of 4 phyllo disks, using a second parchment-lined baking sheet.

**3.** Bake the phyllo disks for 5 minutes, or until golden brown and crispy.

**4.** Meanwhile, transfer the rice pudding to a medium bowl and cover with plastic wrap. Microwave for 3 minutes, stirring at 1-minute intervals. If the pudding seems too soupy, place in a sieve and drain off about ½ cup liquid.

**5.** Divide the pudding among four bowls. Place a scoop of ice cream in the center of each pudding, place a phyllo disk on top, and serve immediately.

# APPLE PAN CRUMBLE

**Number of Servings: 4**  *Estimated Cost: $9.75*

**2 (15-ounce) jars baked apples**
*½ cup packed brown sugar*
**1 cup flour**
**1¼ teaspoons ground cinnamon**
**½ cup minute rolled oats**
*½ teaspoon salt*
*8 tablespoons (1 stick) cold butter, cut into small chunks*

**1.** Pour the apples and their liquid into a medium bowl. Microwave for about 3 minutes, or until heated through.

**2.** Meanwhile, heat two large nonstick sauté pans over medium heat. In a medium bowl, combine the brown sugar, flour, cinnamon, oats, and salt. Add the butter and cut it into the dry ingredients with two forks until the mixture resembles coarse meal.

**3.** Divide the oat mixture between the two hot pans and cook very slowly for 5 minutes, stirring often to ensure even browning and crisping. Transfer to a large plate to cool and harden for a few minutes.

**4.** Spoon the apple mixture into four bowls. Sprinkle the oat crumble liberally on top. Serve immediately.

# BABA AU RUM

**Number of Servings: 4**  *Estimated Cost: $5.50*

¼ cup sugar
2 tablespoons water
**⅔ cup rum**
**4 original glazed Krispy Kreme doughnuts or other glazed doughnuts**
**⅔ cup very cold heavy cream**

**1.** Combine the sugar and water in a small saucepan and bring to a boil over high heat, stirring to dissolve the sugar. Turn off the heat and stir in the rum.

**2.** With a serrated knife, carefully split each doughnut in half. With a pastry brush, heavily soak the cut side of each half with the rum syrup.

**3.** In a medium bowl, whip the cream until stiff peaks form.

**4.** Spoon one-quarter of the whipped cream onto the bottom half of each doughnut. Sandwich the 2 halves together to form a doughnut sandwich, and serve.

# BUTTERSCOTCH CHOCOLATE FONDUE WITH GRAHAM CRACKERS AND BANANA

**Number of Servings: 4**  *Estimated Cost: $9.75*

1 (17.5-ounce) jar butterscotch sauce
2 ounces unsweetened chocolate, finely chopped
3 tablespoons scotch
20 graham crackers
2 ripe bananas, peeled and cut into 1-inch chunks

**1.** In a fondue pot, bring the butterscotch sauce to a boil. Turn down the heat and whisk in the chocolate until melted. Stir in the scotch.

**2.** Serve the fondue with the graham crackers and the bananas for dipping.

# CHOCOLATE CAKES WITH RASPBERRIES AND NUTELLA MOUSSE

**Number of Servings: 4**  *Estimated Cost: $15.50*

**2½ pints fresh raspberries**
*2 tablespoons sugar*
*1 teaspoon white vinegar*
**¼ cup Nutella**
**1 cup very cold heavy cream**
*Pinch of salt*
**4 mini chocolate cake shells (about 3½ inches in diameter)**

**1.** In a medium bowl, combine two-thirds of the raspberries with the sugar and vinegar. Mash the raspberries with a fork until the juices are released and the mixture becomes a very coarse puree. Set aside.

**2.** Combine the Nutella, cream, and salt in a medium bowl and beat until medium-stiff peaks form; be careful not to overwhip the cream.

**3.** Fill the cake shells with the raspberry mixture. Mound the Nutella mousse on top. Scatter the remaining raspberries over the tops of the desserts. Serve immediately, or chill, if desired.

# CLASSIC CANNOLI

**Number of Servings: 4** *Estimated Cost: $12*

**1 (15-ounce) container whole-milk ricotta cheese**
**½ cup mascarpone cheese**
**⅓ cup orange marmalade**
*⅔ cup confectioners' sugar*
*Pinch of salt*
**8 large cannoli shells (LaRosa makes good ones)**
**Chocolate chips for sprinkling**

**1.** In the bowl of an electric mixer (or another large bowl), combine the ricotta, mascarpone, and orange marmalade. Beat with the wire whip attachment (or regular beaters), until smooth, about 1 minute. Slowly add the sugar and salt and beat until combined.

**2.** Fill a pastry bag fitted with a large plain tip with the cheese mixture. Pipe the mixture, working from both ends, to fill each cannoli shell. Sprinkle the chocolate chips onto the cheese mixture peeking out of each end of the cannoli. Serve immediately, or refrigerate until serving time.

# CRISPY GOLDEN CROISSANTS WITH PUMPKIN CREAM AND CANDIED GINGER

**Number of Servings: 4**  *Estimated Cost: $7*

¾ cup sugar
1½ teaspoons ground cinnamon
4 medium croissants, split
1 cup very cold heavy cream
¾ cup canned pumpkin puree, chilled
4 pieces crystallized ginger, cut into thin strips

**1.** Preheat a toaster oven to high or turn on the oven broiler.

**2.** Combine the sugar and 1 teaspoon cinnamon and pour onto a plate. Dip each croissant into the cinnamon sugar, coating it well. Place the croissants in the toaster oven or under the broiler and toast until golden brown, about 3 minutes. Let cool.

**3.** Meanwhile, in a medium bowl, combine the cream, pumpkin puree, the remaining ½ teaspoon cinnamon, and ¼ cup of the remaining cinnamon sugar and beat with an electric mixer until the mixture is slightly stiff and airy. (You can do this up to 3 hours ahead; chill.)

**4.** To assemble, place each croissant cut side up on a plate. Spoon the pumpkin cream onto the croissants. Sprinkle the crystallized ginger on top, and serve immediately.

# DUTCH APPLES ON CHALLAH WITH MAPLE-WALNUT SAUCE

**Number of Servings: 4**  *Estimated Cost: $11.50*

*4 tablespoons butter, softened*
**4 (¾-inch) slices challah bread**
**1¼ cups walnut halves, coarsely crushed**
**1 cup heavy cream**
**½ cup maple syrup**
*Salt*
**1 (15-ounce) jar baked apples**

**1.** Preheat the oven to 450 degrees. Preheat a toaster oven to high or turn on the oven broiler.

**2.** Spread the butter on both sides of each slice of challah. Place in the toaster oven or under the broiler and toast until golden brown and crisp on the outside. Set aside.

**3.** Spread the walnuts on a baking sheet and bake in the oven for 5 minutes, or until fragrant and toasted. Set aside.

**4.** Meanwhile, heat a large sauté pan over high heat until hot. Add the cream; it will boil vigorously. Boil until reduced and extremely thick, then stir in the maple syrup. Add the nuts. Season with a little salt. Keep warm.

**5.** In a medium bowl, microwave the apples in their liquid until hot, about 2 minutes. To serve, place a piece of challah in the center of each plate. Top with apples, using their liquid to soak the bread. Spoon the maple-walnut mixture on top.

# GUAVA TAPIOCA WITH MACADAMIA NUTS

**Number of Servings: 4** *Estimated Cost: $7.75*

½ cup instant tapioca
2 cups guava nectar, plus more as needed
*Pinch of salt*
½ cup macadamia pieces
2 small ripe starfruit, thinly sliced
1¼ cups passion fruit sorbet

**1.** Combine the tapioca and guava nectar in a medium saucepan, off the heat. Let sit for 5 minutes.

**2.** Cook the tapioca, stirring constantly, until tender, about 3 minutes. Add more guava nectar to thin if necessary, and season with the salt.

**3.** To serve, spoon the tapioca into four bowls and scatter the macadamia pieces on top. Arrange the starfruit slices on top of the tapioca and place a scoop of passion fruit sorbet in the center of each. Serve immediately.

# FRESH ORANGES WITH JACK DANIEL'S AND YOGURT

**Number of Servings: 4**  *Estimated Cost: $7*

*4 tablespoons butter*
*⅓ cup sugar*
**6 oranges, peeled and separated into segments, juice reserved**
**¼ cup Jack Daniel's Tennessee Whiskey**
*Pinch of salt*
**1⅓ cups vanilla yogurt**

**1.** Heat a large sauté pan over high heat until smoking. Add the butter, sugar, and reserved orange juice. Bring to a boil and boil to reduce until slightly syrupy, about 1½ minutes.

**2.** Turn off the heat and stir in the whiskey. Add the orange segments to the pan, season with the salt, and toss gently to coat.

**3.** Divide the orange mixture among four bowls and top each bowl with ⅓ cup of the yogurt. Serve.

# PINEAPPLE FRENCH TOAST

**Number of Servings: 4**  *Estimated Cost: $13.75*

**8 thin slices challah bread**
**½ fresh pineapple (you can buy one already cored, peeled, and thinly sliced, but be sure to reserve the juice)**
*8 tablespoons (1 stick) butter*
**4 eggs**
*3 tablespoons sugar*
*2 tablespoons water*
*Pinch of salt*
**1½ teaspoons Chinese 5-spice powder**
**1 pint vanilla ice cream**

**1.** Place 4 slices of challah on a work surface and lay the pineapple slices in a single layer on top of each piece. Top with the remaining bread and press down firmly.

**2.** Melt the butter in a very large nonstick sauté pan. Meanwhile, blend the eggs, sugar, water, salt, and 5-spice powder in a shallow dish. Dip the sandwiches in the mixture, turning to coat completely.

**3.** When the butter is foaming, place the sandwiches in the pan. Cook for about 2½ minutes per side, or until golden brown. Remove from the pan and place on plates.

**4.** Add ⅓ cup of the reserved pineapple juice to the pan, bring to a boil, and boil until reduced, thick, and syrupy.

**5.** Spoon some of the sauce over the French toast, top each with a scoop of vanilla ice cream, and serve.

# CROISSANTS WITH PRUNES AND ARMAGNAC

**Number of Servings: 4** *Estimated Cost: $11.75*

4 medium croissants, split
*Sugar*
20 pitted prunes (about 1 cup), roughly chopped
1 cup butterscotch sauce
¼ cup Armagnac
1 lemon, scrubbed

**1.** Preheat a toaster oven to high or turn on the oven broiler. Dip the cut side of the croissants in sugar. Place in the toaster oven or under the broiler and toast until golden brown and crispy, about 3 minutes; watch the croissants carefully so they don't burn.

**2.** Meanwhile, in a medium saucepan, combine the prunes and butterscotch and bring to a boil. Lower the heat and simmer for about 3 minutes, stirring frequently. Remove from the heat, add the Armagnac, and stir to blend.

**3.** To serve, place a croissant on each plate. Spoon the butterscotch prune sauce liberally over and around. Zest the lemon directly over each plate, being careful to disperse the zest evenly. Serve with vanilla ice cream, if desired.

# THAI BLING-BLING SOUP

**Number of Servings: 4**  *Estimated Cost: $7.50*

**2 cups prepared tapioca pudding**
**½ cup Coco Lopez cream of coconut**
*⅓ cup water*
**4 Jell-O Sugar Free Gelatin Snacks (2 peach, 2 watermelon)**
**or other prepared gelatin**
**4 Flav-O-Ice pops (2 green, 2 blue) or other frozen fruit pops**

**1.** Combine the tapioca pudding, cream of coconut, and water in a bowl and stir until blended. Divide among four bowls.

**2.** Cut the gelatin into large dice. Cut the pops into 1-inch pieces. Scatter the Jell-O cubes and Flav-O-Ice pieces over the tapioca in each bowl. Serve immediately.

# WARM BROWNIES WITH A SALTY PEANUT SAUCE

**Number of Servings: 4**  *Estimated Cost: $12.00*

⅓ **cup peanut butter**
⅜ **cup heavy cream**
*¼ cup water*
*Pinch of salt*
**4 (4-ounce) commercially prepared brownies**
½ **cup salted peanuts**
**2 cups vanilla ice cream**

**1.** In a small saucepot, heat the first 4 ingredients, stirring constantly with a whisk. Bring to a simmer and turn off heat, thin with more water if necessary.

**2.** Microwave the brownies for 30 seconds, or until warm. Spoon sauce over brownies and sprinkle with peanuts. Top with vanilla ice cream and serve immediately.

# INDEX

achiote, Good Ol' Rice and Beans, 118
Alfredo sauce
    Roast Beef and Eggplant Alfredo, 220
    Turkey Chopped Steak with Peas and
        Pickled Onions, 201
All-Purpose Mushroom Mix, 115
anchovies, Capellini alla Puttanesca, 139
Andouille Sausage Jambalaya with
    Clams and Peas, 231
Angel Food and Cherry Cake with
    Ginger Cream, 248
apple jelly, Boneless Pork Chops with
    Potato Pancakes and Mustard
    Greens, 237
apples, baked
    Apple Pan Crumble, 264
    Dutch Apples on Challah with Maple-
        Walnut Sauce, 270
apples, fresh, Warm Waldorf Chicken
    Salad, 88
Apricot and Dried Cherry Pound Cake,
    249
Armagnac, Croissants with Prunes and
    Armagnac, 274
artichoke hearts
    Chilled Pork Tenderloin Salad with
        Chopped Olive Dressing, 89
    Fried Calamari and Artichokes with
        Hummus Dipping Sauce, 36
    Ham on Rye with Artichokes and
        Dijon, 102
    Veal Scaloppini in Artichoke Broth, 227
    Warm Artichoke Parmigiano Dip, 29
arugula
    Chilled Pork Tenderloin Salad with
        Chopped Olive Dressing, 89
    Crab Cakes with Avocado Dip and
        Arugula Salad, 178
    Golden Chicken and Taleggio Cutlets,
        197
    Prosciutto, Parmigiano, Pimiento, and
        Arugula Salad, 90
    Roast Beef Wrap with Garlic Relish, 101
asparagus
    Grilled Asparagus and Oyster
        Mushrooms with Pecorino Cheese,
        30
    Soft Scrambled Eggs with Asparagus
        on Toasted Croissants, 127
avocado dip, prepared, Crab Cakes with
    Avocado Dip and Arugula Salad, 178

avocados
    Avocado Salad with Red Onion and
        Feta, 76
    Fresh Fast Guacamole, 26
    Pico de Gallo Salad with Avocado, 77

Baba au Rum, 265
bacon
    Linguine alla Carbonara, 147
    Shrimp and Noodle Saté Sauté, 183
bananas
    Butterscotch Chocolate Fondue with
        Graham Crackers and Banana, 266
    Caramelized Banana Panini, 251
barbecue sauce
    Barbecue Kielbasa with Corn, Black
        Beans, and Corn Muffins, 232
    Salmon in Butternut Squash Barbecue
        Sauce, 167
basil
    Apricot and Dried Cherry Pound Cake,
        249
    Basil and Potato Frittata with Frisée,
        124
    Beef and Broccoli-Coleslaw Stir-Fry,
        214
    Chicken and Cauliflower Flash-Fry,
        190
    Chicken with Tomato, Basil, and
        Crispy Parmigiano Crackers, 194
    Duck and Eggplant Flash-Fry, 207
    Grilled Stuffed Veal with Basil and
        Provolone, 47
    Mamma's Vegetable Giambotta, 119
    Prosciutto, Mozzarella, and Tomato
        Panini, 109
    Puffy Chicken with Green Curry Basil
        Sauce, 46
    Tomato and Mozzarella Salad, 80
    Vietnamese Beef and Basil Soup, 73
    Warm Artichoke Parmigiano Dip, 29
    Warm Chicken, Feta, and Melon Seed
        Pasta Salad, 142
beans, dried. see specific types
beans, fresh, Hot Italian Sausage with
    Fresh Beans and Beets, 234
beans, refried
    Ground Beef with Refried Beans,
        Salsa, and Grilled Zucchini, 224
    Ground Beef with Salsa Verde,
        Radicchio, and Sour Cream, 225

bean sprouts, Turkey, Green Onion, and
    Rice Noodle Soup, 70
beef
    Beef and Broccoli-Coleslaw Stir-Fry,
        214
    Beef and Onion Flash-Fry, 215
    Beef Curry Sauté, 217
    Beef Shabu-Shabu with Watercress, 71
    Beef Swiss Fondue with Three Sauces,
        58
    Beefy Shepherd's Pie, 223
    Broiled Flat-Iron Steaks with Pepper
        Jack Scalloped Potatoes, 211
    Cheesy Roast Beef and Zucchini, 221
    Corned Beef Brisket with Cabbage,
        Potatoes, and Horseradish, 226
    Grilled Flank Steak with Shredded
        Carrots and Pickled Ginger, 213
    Ground Beef with Refried Beans,
        Salsa, and Grilled Zucchini, 224
    Ground Beef with Salsa Verde,
        Radicchio, and Sour Cream, 225
    Mushroom and Red Onion Burgers,
        100
    Quick Steak, Pizza Man Style, 216
    Roast Beef, Chestnuts, and Brussels
        Sprouts in Consommé, 222
    Roast Beef and Boursin Panini, 108
    Roast Beef and Eggplant Alfredo, 220
    Roast Beef Borscht, 72
    Roast Beef Wrap with Garlic Relish,
        101
    Sirloin Tips with Gorgonzola Mashed
        Potatoes, 210
    Vietnamese Beef and Basil Soup, 73
beef gravy, Beefy Shepherd's Pie, 223
Beefy Shepherd's Pie, 223
beer, Sharp Cheddar and Beer Fondue
    with Warm Pretzels, 50
beets
    Hot Italian Sausage with Fresh Beans
        and Beets, 234
    Roast Beef Borscht, 72
    Sautéed Pork with Snow Peas,
        Walnuts, and Beets, 240
Black-and-Tan Salmon with Scallions,
    165
black beans
    Barbecue Kielbasa with Corn, Black
        Beans, and Corn Muffins, 232
    Good Ol' Rice and Beans, 118

black bean sauce, Pork and Zucchini Flash-Fry with Black Bean Sauce, 239
black bean soup, prepared, Black-and-Tan Salmon with Scallions, 165
blackberries
    Blueberry Pomegranate Consommé with Whipped Crème Fraîche, 250
    Cocoa Cookies with Black Raspberry Ice Cream and Chocolate Fudge, 255
Blueberry Pomegranate Consommé with Whipped Crème Fraîche, 250
blue cheese, Buffalo Chicken Tenders with Celery and Blue Cheese Salad, 85
bok choy, Handkerchief Pasta with Lobster, Bok Choy, and Lemon Cream Sauce, 141
Boneless Pork Chops with Potato Pancakes and Mustard Greens, 237
Borscht, Roast Beef, 72
Bouillon, Rich Mushroom, 63
Boursin cheese
    Mushroom Soup with Boursin Croutons, 64
    Roast Beef and Boursin Panini, 108
    Stuffed Pork Chops with Boursin and Collards, 242
bread crumbs
    Clams Oreganata, 37
    Cod Provençal, 159
    Duck Swiss Fondue, 57
    Eggplant Parmigiano, 125
    Firecracker Shrimp, 39
    Garlicky Lemon Shrimp, 41
    Roast Beef and Eggplant Alfredo, 220
    Stuffed Pork Chops with Boursin and Collards, 242
bread sticks, Beef Swiss Fondue with Three Sauces, 58
Brie cheese, Hot Chicken and Brie Sandwich with Toasted Pecans, 94
broccoli
    Shrimp and Broccoli Flash-Fry, 180
    Turkey, Broccoli, and Cheese Casserole, 206
broccoli coleslaw
    Beef and Broccoli-Coleslaw Stir-Fry, 214
    Pork Scaloppini Stuffed with Cheddar, 238
broccoli rabe
    Parmigiano Chicken with Molten Provolone, 198
    Shrimp Fra Diavolo with Couscous and Broccoli Rabe, 182
Broiled Flat-Iron Steaks with Pepper Jack Scalloped Potatoes, 211
brussels sprouts, Roast Beef, Chestnuts, and Brussels Sprouts in Consommé, 222

Buffalo Chicken Tenders with Celery and Blue Cheese Salad, 85
buttermilk, Shrimp Swiss Fondue with Arrabbiata Dipping Sauce, 54
butternut squash puree, Trout with Butternut Squash and Blood Oranges, 162–63
butternut squash soup, Salmon in Butternut Squash Barbecue Sauce, 167
butterscotch sauce
    Butterscotch Chocolate Fondue with Graham Crackers and Banana, 266
    Croissants with Prunes and Armagnac, 274

cabbage, coleslaw mix, Corned Beef Brisket with Cabbage, Potatoes, and Horseradish, 226
cabbage, Napa, Salmon with Shiitake Mushrooms in Ginger-Soy Broth, 168
cabbage, sauerkraut
    Kielbasa and Sauerkraut Stew, 236
    Toasted Hot Dog Reubin, 103
cabbage, sweet-and-sour red
    Hot Turkey "Coleslaw" Sandwich, 96
    Sautéed Scallops with Pickled Ginger Red Cabbage, 179
cakes
    Angel Food and Cherry Cake with Ginger Cream, 248
    Apricot and Dried Cherry Pound Cake, 249
    Chocolate Cakes with Raspberries and Nutella Mousse, 267
cannellini beans
    Cannellini with Tricolor Peppers, Tomato, and Parsley, 116
    Parmigiano Flounder with White Beans and Olive Tapenade, 155
    Skewered Shrimp with Beans and Scallions, 187
    White Bean and Mushroom Chili, 129
Cannoli, Classic, 268
Capellini alla Puttanesca, 139
Capellini with Littleneck Clams, 136
capers
    Capellini alla Puttanesca, 139
    Chicken with Lemon, Capers, and Red Onions, 196
Caramelized Banana Panini, 251
caramel sauce, Pears in Phyllo Cups with Butter Pecan Ice Cream and Caramel Sauce, 260
carrots
    Grilled Flank Steak with Shredded Carrots and Pickled Ginger, 213
    Honey-Glazed Salmon with Cinnamon, Carrots, and Chicory, 166

Casserole, Turkey, Broccoli, and Cheese, 206
Catfish and Rice Sofrito, 175
cauliflower, Chicken and Cauliflower Flash-Fry, 190
celery hearts
    Buffalo Chicken Tenders with Celery and Blue Cheese Salad, 85
    Smoked Salmon and Swiss Cheese Panini, 107
    Warm Waldorf Chicken Salad, 88
celery leaves
    Goat Cheese, Radish, and Dried Cranberry Salad, 78
    See-Thru Scallops with Lemon Brown Butter and Celery Leaves, 42
challah bread
    Caramelized Banana Panini, 251
    Dutch Apples on Challah with Maple-Walnut Sauce, 270
    Pineapple French Toast, 273
chard, Miso-Walnut Chicken with Rainbow Swiss Chard, 200
Charred Mackerel with Pears and Caesar Dressing, 81
cheddar cheese
    Beefy Shepherd's Pie, 223
    Mushroom Quesadillas, 33
    Pork Scaloppini Stuffed with Cheddar, 238
    Pretzelized Chicken with Cheddar Horseradish Sauce, 199
    Sharp Cheddar and Beer Fondue with Warm Pretzels, 50
cheddar cheese soup, Turkey, Broccoli, and Cheese Casserole, 206
cheddar crackers, Pork Scaloppini Stuffed with Cheddar, 238
cheese. see specific types
Cheesy Roast Beef and Zucchini, 221
cherries, dried, Apricot and Dried Cherry Pound Cake, 249
cherry pie filling, Angel Food and Cherry Cake with Ginger Cream, 248
cherry preserves, Angel Food and Cherry Cake with Ginger Cream, 248
chestnuts
    Roast Beef, Chestnuts, and Brussels Sprouts in Consommé, 222
    Sea Bass with Leeks, Chestnuts, and Dates, 156
chicken
    Buffalo Chicken Tenders with Celery and Blue Cheese Salad, 85
    Chicken, Goat Cheese, and Blood Orange Salad, 84
    Chicken and Cauliflower Flash-Fry, 190
    Chicken and Chopped Salad, 87
    Chicken and Wild Mushroom Strudel, 192

chicken (cont.)
   Chicken Swiss Fondue with Dijon Sour
      Cream and Hummus, 56
   Chicken with Lemon, Capers, and Red
      Onions, 196
   Chicken with Tomato, Basil, and
      Crispy Parmigiano Crackers, 194
   Golden Chicken and Taleggio Cutlets,
      197
   Hot Chicken and Brie Sandwich with
      Toasted Pecans, 94
   Miso-Walnut Chicken with Rainbow
      Swiss Chard, 200
   Parmigiano Chicken with Molten
      Provolone, 198
   Peanut Chicken and Radicchio Salad,
      86
   Pretzelized Chicken with Cheddar
      Horseradish Sauce, 199
   Puffy Chicken with Green Curry Basil
      Sauce, 46
   Warm Chicken, Feta, and Melon Seed
      Pasta Salad, 142
   Warm Waldorf Chicken Salad, 88
chicken livers, Fennel-Seared Chicken
      Livers with Watercress and
      Oranges, 44
chicory, Honey-Glazed Salmon with
      Cinnamon, Carrots, and Chicory, 166
Chili, White Bean and Mushroom, 129
chili paste, Shrimp Fra Diavolo with
      Couscous and Broccoli Rabe, 182
Chilled Cucumber Soup with Smoked
      Salmon and Crème Fraîche, 62
Chilled Pork Tenderloin Salad with
      Chopped Olive Dressing, 89
chives
   Corn and Crab Chowder with
      Tarragon, 66
   Grilled Asparagus and Oyster
      Mushrooms with Pecorino Cheese,
      30
   Hot Italian Sausage with Fresh Beans
      and Beets, 234
   Mushroom Soup with Boursin
      Croutons, 64
   Pear and Stilton Salad, 79
   Rich Mushroom Bouillon, 63
   See-Thru Scallops with Lemon Brown
      Butter and Celery Leaves, 42
   Sole with Charred Red Onions and
      Lemon Butter, 152
chocolate
   Butterscotch Chocolate Fondue with
      Graham Crackers and Banana, 266
   Chocolate Cakes with Raspberries and
      Nutella Mousse, 267
   Chocolate Phyllo with Blood Oranges
      and Dulce de Leche Ice Cream, 254
   Cocoa Cookies with Black Raspberry
      Ice Cream and Chocolate Fudge, 255

chocolate (cont.)
   Doughnuts and Hot Chocolate, 256
   Grilled Pineapple with Cocoa Foam,
      257
   S'Mores Tartlets, 262
   Warm Brownies with a Salty Peanut
      Sauce, 276
Chorizo, Smoked Mussel, and Okra Rice
      Pilaf, 235
Chorizo and Manchego Frittata with
      Mesclun Salad, 233
chutney, Black-and-Tan Salmon with
      Scallions, 165
cilantro
   Avocado Salad with Red Onion and
      Feta, 76
   Beef and Onion Flash-Fry, 215
   Fresh Fast Guacamole, 26
   Good Ol' Rice and Beans, 118
   Grilled Flank Steak with Shredded
      Carrots and Pickled Ginger, 213
   Grilled Squid with Coconut Broth,
      Leeks, and Papaya, 171
   Hot-and-Sour Shrimp Rice Noodle
      Soup, 69
   Pico de Gallo Salad with Avocado,
      77
   Rice Noodles with Spicy Peanut
      Sauce, 134
   Shrimp and Broccoli Flash-Fry, 180
   Shrimp Salad with Red Onion, Mango,
      and Cilantro, 82
cilantro seasoning, Chorizo, Smoked
      Mussel, and Okra Rice Pilaf, 235
clam juice, Capellini with Littleneck
      Clams, 136
clams
   Andouille Sausage Jambalaya with
      Clams and Peas, 231
   Capellini with Littleneck Clams, 136
   Clam Brodettatto with Chorizo and
      Peas, 176
   Clams Oreganata, 37
Classic Cannoli, 268
Cocoa Cookies with Black Raspberry
      Ice Cream and Chocolate Fudge,
      255
coconut, cream of, Thai Bling-Bling
      Soup, 275
coconut curry marinade, Puffy Chicken
      with Green Curry Basil Sauce, 46
coconut ginger soup, prepared, Grilled
      Squid with Coconut Broth, Leeks,
      and Papaya, 171
coconut milk
   Beef Curry Sauté, 217
   Curried Mussel Fricassee, 177
cod
   Cod Flash-Fry with Mint, 158
   Cod Provençal, 159
   Red, White, and Green Cod, 160

collard greens
   Gnocchi with Toasted Garlic, Walnuts,
      and Bitter Greens, 135
   Stuffed Pork Chops with Boursin and
      Collards, 242
Cookies, Cocoa, with Black Raspberry
      Ice Cream and Chocolate Fudge,
      255
Corn and Crab Chowder with Tarragon,
      66
Corned Beef Brisket with Cabbage,
      Potatoes, and Horseradish, 226
Cornmeal and Red Onion–Crusted Skate
      with Lime Butter, 164
corn muffins, Barbecue Kielbasa with
      Corn, Black Beans, and Corn
      Muffins, 232
couscous, Shrimp Fra Diavolo with
      Couscous and Broccoli Rabe, 182
crabmeat
   Corn and Crab Chowder with
      Tarragon, 66
   Crab Cakes with Avocado Dip and
      Arugula Salad, 178
cranberries, dried
   Goat Cheese, Radish, and Dried
      Cranberry Salad, 78
   Grilled Lamb with Sweet-and-Sour
      Cranberry Sauce, 245
cream, heavy
   Angel Food and Cherry Cake with
      Ginger Cream, 248
   Baba au Rum, 265
   Broiled Flat-Iron Steaks with Pepper
      Jack Scalloped Potatoes, 211
   Chocolate Cakes with Raspberries and
      Nutella Mousse, 267
   Crispy Golden Croissants with
      Pumpkin Cream and Candied
      Ginger, 269
   Crispy Wonton Wafers with Lemon
      Curd and Strawberries, 259
   Dutch Apples on Challah with Maple-
      Walnut Sauce, 270
   Scalloped Potatoes with Gruyère
      Cheese and Mushrooms, 120
   Sirloin Tips with Gorgonzola Mashed
      Potatoes, 210
   Warm Brownies with a Salty Peanut
      Sauce, 276
Creamy Lemon Shrimp Salad with
      Cucumbers and Watercress, 35
crème fraîche
   Blueberry Pomegranate Consommé
      with Whipped Crème Fraîche, 250
   Chilled Cucumber Soup with Smoked
      Salmon and Crème Fraîche, 62
   Handkerchief Pasta with Lobster, Bok
      Choy, and Lemon Cream Sauce, 141
Crispy Golden Croissants with Pumpkin
      Cream and Candied Ginger, 269

Crispy Wonton Wafers with Lemon Curd and Strawberries, 259
croissants
Crispy Golden Croissants with Pumpkin Cream and Candied Ginger, 269
Croissants with Prunes and Armagnac, 274
Soft Scrambled Eggs with Asparagus on Toasted Croissants, 127
cucumbers
Chilled Cucumber Soup with Smoked Salmon and Crème Fraîche, 62
Creamy Lemon Shrimp Salad with Cucumbers and Watercress, 35
Grilled Boneless Leg of Lamb with Greek Yogurt Sauce, 244
Curried Mussel Fricassee, 177

dandelion greens, Pierogi with Ham, Dandelion Greens, and Sour Cream Mustard Sauce, 145
dates, Sea Bass with Leeks, Chestnuts, and Dates, 156
Dijonnaise, Chicken and Chopped Salad, 87
dill, Chilled Cucumber Soup with Smoked Salmon and Crème Fraîche, 62
dips
Crab Cakes with Avocado Dip and Arugula Salad, 178
Fresh Fast Guacamole, 26
Warm Artichoke Parmigiano Dip, 29
doughnuts
Baba au Rum, 265
Doughnuts and Hot Chocolate, 256
duck
Duck and Eggplant Flash-Fry, 207
Duck Swiss Fondue, 57
duck sauce, Duck Swiss Fondue, 57
Dutch Apples on Challah with Maple-Walnut Sauce, 270

eggplant
Duck and Eggplant Flash-Fry, 207
Eggplant Parmigiano, 125
Roast Beef and Eggplant Alfredo, 220
eggs
Basil and Potato Frittata with Frisée, 124
Chicken and Cauliflower Flash-Fry, 190
Chorizo and Manchego Frittata with Mesclun Salad, 233
Duck and Eggplant Flash-Fry, 207
Golden Chicken and Taleggio Cutlets, 197
Linguine alla Carbonara, 147
Pineapple French Toast, 273
Red Onion Frittata with Baby Spinach, 126
Shrimp and Broccoli Flash-Fry, 180

eggs (cont.)
Shrimp and Scallion Frittata, 181
Soft Scrambled Eggs with Asparagus on Toasted Croissants, 127
Stracciatella, 65
Tofu and Red Pepper Flash-Fry, 128
12 Eggs in a Pan, 230
endive
Honey-Glazed Salmon with Cinnamon, Carrots, and Chicory, 166
Mahi-Mahi with Endive and Orange Marmalade Glaze, 170
escarole, Stracciatella, 65

fennel bulbs
Feta and Kalamata Panini, 106
Ham and Gorgonzola Panini, 110
fennel seeds, Fennel-Seared Chicken Livers with Watercress and Oranges, 44
feta cheese
Avocado Salad with Red Onion and Feta, 76
Feta and Kalamata Panini, 106
Warm Chicken, Feta, and Melon Seed Pasta Salad, 142
Firecracker Shrimp, 39
fish sauce, Hot-and-Sour Shrimp Rice Noodle Soup, 69
5-spice powder, Pineapple French Toast, 273
flash-fry dishes
Beef and Onion Flash-Fry, 215
Chicken and Cauliflower Flash-Fry, 190
Cod Flash-Fry with Mint, 158
Duck and Eggplant Flash-Fry, 207
Pork and Zucchini Flash-Fry with Black Bean Sauce, 239
Shrimp and Broccoli Flash-Fry, 180
Tofu and Red Pepper Flash-Fry, 128
see also stir-fry dishes
flounder, Parmigiano Flounder with White Beans and Olive Tapenade, 155
fondues
Beef Swiss Fondue with Three Sauces, 58
Butterscotch Chocolate Fondue with Graham Crackers and Banana, 266
Chicken Swiss Fondue with Dijon Sour Cream and Hummus, 56
Duck Swiss Fondue, 57
Mushroom Fondue, 51
Pigs in a Blanket Swiss Fondue, 59
Salmon and Sesame Swiss Fondue, 52
Sharp Cheddar and Beer Fondue with Warm Pretzels, 50
Shrimp Swiss Fondue with Arrabbiata Dipping Sauce, 54
Tuna Tempura Swiss Fondue with Wasabi Soy, 53

fra diavolo sauce
Capellini alla Puttanesca, 139
Eggplant Parmigiano, 125
Savory Seafood Stew, 174
Shrimp Swiss Fondue with Arrabbiata Dipping Sauce, 54
French Toast, Pineapple, 273
Fresh Fast Guacamole, 26
Fresh Oranges with Jack Daniel's and Yogurt, 272
Fried Calamari and Artichokes with Hummus Dipping Sauce, 36
frisée
Basil and Potato Frittata with Frisée, 124
Pear and Stilton Salad, 79
frittatas
Basil and Potato Frittata with Frisée, 124
Chorizo and Manchego Frittata with Mesclun Salad, 233
Red Onion Frittata with Baby Spinach, 126
Shrimp and Scallion Frittata, 181
Froot Loops cereal, Blueberry Pomegranate Consommé with Whipped Crème Fraîche, 250
frozen fruit pops, Thai Bling-Bling Soup, 275

Garlicky Lemon Shrimp, 41
garlic rib sauce
Grilled Flank Steak with Shredded Carrots and Pickled Ginger, 213
Skewered Shrimp with Beans and Scallions, 187
Tofu and Red Pepper Flash-Fry, 128
gelatin snacks, Thai Bling-Bling Soup, 275
General Tso's sauce, Cod Flash-Fry with Mint, 158
ginger, crystallized, Crispy Golden Croissants with Pumpkin Cream and Candied Ginger, 269
ginger, fresh
Angel Food and Cherry Cake with Ginger Cream, 248
Salmon with Shiitake Mushrooms in Ginger-Soy Broth, 168
ginger, pickled
Grilled Flank Steak with Shredded Carrots and Pickled Ginger, 213
Sautéed Scallops with Pickled Ginger Red Cabbage, 179
ginger sesame sauce, Shrimp and Broccoli Flash-Fry, 180
Gnocchi with Toasted Garlic, Walnuts, and Bitter Greens, 135
goat cheese
Chicken, Goat Cheese, and Blood Orange Salad, 84
Goat Cheese, Radish, and Dried Cranberry Salad, 78

Golden Chicken and Taleggio Cutlets, 197
Good Ol' Rice and Beans, 118
Gorgonzola cheese
    Ham and Gorgonzola Panini, 110
    Sirloin Tips with Gorgonzola Mashed
        Potatoes, 210
graham cracker piecrusts/tartlet shells,
    S'Mores Tartlets, 262
graham crackers, Butterscotch
    Chocolate Fondue with Graham
    Crackers and Banana, 266
greens, bitter. see broccoli rabe; chard;
    dandelion greens; escarole; frisée;
    kale; mustard greens; spinach;
    turnip greens; watercress
greens, salad. see arugula; entries begin-
    ning with "lettuce"; radicchio;
    spinach
Grilled Asparagus and Oyster
    Mushrooms with Pecorino Cheese,
    30
Grilled Boneless Leg of Lamb with Greek
    Yogurt Sauce, 244
Grilled Flank Steak with Shredded
    Carrots and Pickled Ginger, 213
Grilled Lamb with Sweet-and-Sour
    Cranberry Sauce, 245
Grilled Pineapple with Cocoa Foam, 257
Grilled Squid with Coconut Broth, Leeks,
    and Papaya, 171
Grilled Stuffed Veal with Basil and
    Provolone, 47
Ground Beef with Refried Beans, Salsa,
    and Grilled Zucchini, 224
Ground Beef with Salsa Verde,
    Radicchio, and Sour Cream, 225
gruyère cheese
    Mushroom Fondue, 51
    Scalloped Potatoes with Gruyère
    Cheese and Mushrooms, 120
Guacamole, Fresh Fast, 26
Guava Tapioca with Macadamia Nuts, 271

ham
    Ham and Gorgonzola Panini, 110
    Ham on Rye with Artichokes and
        Dijon, 102
    Pierogi with Ham, Dandelion Greens,
        and Sour Cream Mustard Sauce, 145
Handkerchief Pasta with Lobster, Bok
    Choy, and Lemon Cream Sauce, 141
herring in sour cream, Seared Salmon
    with Sugar Snap Peas and Herring,
    169
honey
    Honey-Glazed Salmon with Cinnamon,
        Carrots, and Chicory, 166
    Hot Turkey "Coleslaw" Sandwich, 96
horseradish, Corned Beef Brisket with
    Cabbage, Potatoes, and
    Horseradish, 226

horseradish cheddar cheese spread,
    Pretzelized Chicken with Cheddar
    Horseradish Sauce, 199
horseradish with beets, Roast Beef
    Borscht, 72
Hot-and-Sour Shrimp Rice Noodle Soup,
    69
Hot Chicken and Brie Sandwich with
    Toasted Pecans, 94
hot dogs
    Pigs in a Blanket Swiss Fondue, 59
    Toasted Hot Dog Reubin, 103
Hot Italian Sausage with Fresh Beans
    and Beets, 234
Hot Turkey "Coleslaw" Sandwich, 96
hummus, prepared
    Chicken Swiss Fondue with Dijon Sour
        Cream and Hummus, 56
    Fried Calamari and Artichokes with
        Hummus Dipping Sauce, 36
    Mussels with Hummus Broth and
        Crusty Italian Bread, 38

ice cream
    Apricot and Dried Cherry Pound Cake,
        249
    Caramelized Banana Panini, 251
    Chocolate Phyllo with Blood Oranges
        and Dulce de Leche Ice Cream, 254
    Cocoa Cookies with Black Raspberry
        Ice Cream and Chocolate Fudge,
        255
    Instant Tiramisu with Raspberries, 258
    Pears in Phyllo Cups with Butter
        Pecan Ice Cream and Caramel
        Sauce, 260
    Pineapple French Toast, 273
    Pretty Peach Melba, 261
    Warm Brownies with a Salty Peanut
        Sauce, 276
    Warm Rice Pudding with Rum Raisin
        Ice Cream, 263
Instant Tiramisu with Raspberries, 258

kale, Shrimp and Noodle Saté Sauté,
    183
ketchup, Pigs in a Blanket Swiss Fondue,
    59
kidney beans, Turkey Cutlets with Red
    Kidney Beans, Garlic Relish, and
    Watercress, 203
Kielbasa and Sauerkraut Stew, 236

ladyfingers, Instant Tiramisu with
    Raspberries, 258
lamb
    Grilled Boneless Leg of Lamb with
        Greek Yogurt Sauce, 244
    Grilled Lamb with Sweet-and-Sour
        Cranberry Sauce, 245
Lasagna, Sausage, 148

leeks
    Grilled Squid with Coconut Broth,
        Leeks, and Papaya, 171
    Sea Bass with Leeks, Chestnuts, and
        Dates, 156
lemon and cilantro cooking sauce, Tangy
    Turkey and Snow Pea Stir-Fry, 202
lemon curd, Crispy Wonton Wafers with
    Lemon Curd and Strawberries, 259
lemons
    Avocado Salad with Red Onion and
        Feta, 76
    Charred Mackerel with Pears and
        Caesar Dressing, 81
    Chicken with Lemon, Capers, and Red
        Onions, 196
    Clams Oreganata, 37
    Crab Cakes with Avocado Dip and
        Arugula Salad, 178
    Creamy Lemon Shrimp Salad with
        Cucumbers and Watercress, 35
    Croissants with Prunes and
        Armagnac, 274
    Garlicky Lemon Shrimp, 41
    Handkerchief Pasta with Lobster,
        Bok Choy, and Lemon Cream Sauce,
        141
    Roast Beef, Chestnuts, and Brussels
        Sprouts in Consommé, 222
    See-Thru Scallops with Lemon Brown
        Butter and Celery Leaves, 42
    Shrimp Fra Diavolo with Couscous
        and Broccoli Rabe, 182
    Shrimp Scampi with Grilled Bread, 186
    Sole with Charred Red Onions and
        Lemon Butter, 152
lentil soup, prepared, Red, White, and
    Green Cod, 160
lettuce, Boston, Pico de Gallo Salad with
    Avocado, 77
lettuce, iceberg, Chicken and Chopped
    Salad, 87
lettuce, mesclun greens
    Chicken, Goat Cheese, and Blood
        Orange Salad, 84
    Chorizo and Manchego Frittata with
        Mesclun Salad, 233
lettuce, romaine mix, Charred Mackerel
    with Pears and Caesar Dressing, 81
limes
    Black-and-Tan Salmon with Scallions,
        165
    Caramelized Banana Panini, 251
    Cornmeal and Red Onion–Crusted
        Skate with Lime Butter, 164
    Good Ol' Rice and Beans, 118
    Pico de Gallo Salad with Avocado, 77
    Shrimp Salad with Red Onion, Mango,
        and Cilantro, 82
    Vietnamese Beef and Basil Soup, 73
Linguine alla Carbonara, 147

lobster, Handkerchief Pasta with Lobster, Bok Choy, and Lemon Cream Sauce, 141

macadamia nuts, Guava Tapioca with Macadamia Nuts, 271
mackerel, Charred Mackerel with Pears and Caesar Dressing, 81
Maggi seasoning, Turkey, Green Onion, and Rice Noodle Soup, 70
Mahi-Mahi with Endive and Orange Marmalade Glaze, 170
Mamma's Vegetable Giambotta, 119
Manchego cheese, Chorizo and Manchego Frittata with Mesclun Salad, 233
mangoes, Shrimp Salad with Red Onion, Mango, and Cilantro, 82
maple syrup, Dutch Apples on Challah with Maple-Walnut Sauce, 270
marinara sauce
    Parmigiano Flounder with White Beans and Olive Tapenade, 155
    Sausage Lasagna, 148
    White Bean and Mushroom Chili, 129
marjoram, Savory Seafood Stew, 174
marshmallow creme, S'Mores Tartlets, 262
mascarpone cheese, Classic Cannoli, 268
menus, sample, 21–23
mint
    Cod Flash-Fry with Mint, 158
    Grilled Boneless Leg of Lamb with Greek Yogurt Sauce, 244
    Pork and Zucchini Flash-Fry with Black Bean Sauce, 239
mirin (rice wine), Shrimp and Scallion Frittata, 181
Miso-Walnut Chicken with Rainbow Swiss Chard, 200
mocha sauce, Instant Tiramisu with Raspberries, 258
mozzarella cheese
    Prosciutto, Mozzarella, and Tomato Panini, 109
    Sausage Lasagna, 148
    Tomato and Mozzarella Salad, 80
    12 Eggs in a Pan, 230
mushrooms
    All-Purpose Mushroom Mix, 115
    Chicken and Wild Mushroom Strudel, 192
    Grilled Asparagus and Oyster Mushrooms with Pecorino Cheese, 30
    Mamma's Vegetable Giambotta, 119
    Mushroom and Red Onion Burgers, 100
    Mushroom Fondue, 51
    Mushroom Quesadillas, 33
    Mushroom Soup with Boursin Croutons, 64

mushrooms (cont.)
    Rich Mushroom Bouillon, 63
    Salmon with Shiitake Mushrooms in Ginger-Soy Broth, 168
    Scalloped Potatoes with Gruyère Cheese and Mushrooms, 120
    Soft Polenta with Wild Mushrooms, 121
    White Bean and Mushroom Chili, 129
mushrooms, marinated, Turkey Chopped Steak with Peas and Pickled Onions, 201
mushroom soup, prepared, Mushroom Soup with Boursin Croutons, 64
mussels
    Curried Mussel Fricassee, 177
    Mussels with Hummus Broth and Crusty Italian Bread, 38
mussels, smoked, Chorizo, Smoked Mussel, and Okra Rice Pilaf, 235
mustard, brown, Pigs in a Blanket Swiss Fondue, 59
mustard, Chinese, Duck Swiss Fondue, 57
mustard, Dijon
    Beef Shabu-Shabu with Watercress, 71
    Boneless Pork Chops with Potato Pancakes and Mustard Greens, 237
    Chicken Swiss Fondue with Dijon Sour Cream and Hummus, 56
    Grilled Lamb with Sweet-and-Sour Cranberry Sauce, 245
    Ham on Rye with Artichokes and Dijon, 102
    Kielbasa and Sauerkraut Stew, 236
    Pierogi with Ham, Dandelion Greens, and Sour Cream Mustard Sauce, 145
    Prosciutto, Parmigiano, Pimiento, and Arugula Salad, 90
mustard greens
    Boneless Pork Chops with Potato Pancakes and Mustard Greens, 237
    Gnocchi with Toasted Garlic, Walnuts, and Bitter Greens, 135

New-Style Tuna Sashimi, 34
noodles. see pasta; rice noodles
Nutella, Chocolate Cakes with Raspberries and Nutella Mousse, 267

oats, Apple Pan Crumble, 264
okra, Chorizo, Smoked Mussel, and Okra Rice Pilaf, 235
olive paste, Fried Calamari and Artichokes with Hummus Dipping Sauce, 36
olives
    Chilled Pork Tenderloin Salad with Chopped Olive Dressing, 89
    Feta and Kalamata Panini, 106

onions, Linguine alla Carbonara, 147
onions, cocktail
    Roast Beef and Boursin Panini, 108
    Turkey Chopped Steak with Peas and Pickled Onions, 201
onions, hot dog
    Beef Swiss Fondue with Three Sauces, 58
    Quick Steak, Pizza Man Style, 216
onions, red
    Avocado Salad with Red Onion and Feta, 76
    Catfish and Rice Sofrito, 175
    Chicken with Lemon, Capers, and Red Onions, 196
    Cornmeal and Red Onion–Crusted Skate with Lime Butter, 164
    Mushroom and Red Onion Burgers, 100
    Red Onion Frittata with Baby Spinach, 126
    Salmon in Butternut Squash Barbecue Sauce, 167
    Shrimp Salad with Red Onion, Mango, and Cilantro, 82
    Sole with Charred Red Onions and Lemon Butter, 152
onions, Vidalia
    Beef and Onion Flash-Fry, 215
    Cod Flash-Fry with Mint, 158
    Ham and Gorgonzola Panini, 110
    Ham on Rye with Artichokes and Dijon, 102
orange marmalade
    Classic Cannoli, 268
    Mahi-Mahi with Endive and Orange Marmalade Glaze, 170
    Miso-Walnut Chicken with Rainbow Swiss Chard, 200
oranges
    Chicken, Goat Cheese, and Blood Orange Salad, 84
    Chocolate Phyllo with Blood Oranges and Dulce de Leche Ice Cream, 254
    Fennel-Seared Chicken Livers with Watercress and Oranges, 44
    Fresh Oranges with Jack Daniel's and Yogurt, 272
    Peanut Chicken and Radicchio Salad, 86
    Trout with Butternut Squash and Blood Oranges, 162–63
oregano
    Clams Oreganata, 37
    Cod Provençal, 159
    Savory Seafood Stew, 174

pad Thai sauce, Chicken and Cauliflower Flash-Fry, 190

panini
    Caramelized Banana Panini, 251
    Feta and Kalamata Panini, 106
    Ham and Gorgonzola Panini, 110
    Prosciutto, Mozzarella, and Tomato
       Panini, 109
    Roast Beef and Boursin Panini, 108
    Smoked Salmon and Swiss Cheese
       Panini, 107
papayas, Grilled Squid with Coconut
    Broth, Leeks, and Papaya, 171
Parmigiano Chicken with Molten
    Provolone, 198
Parmigiano Flounder with White Beans
    and Olive Tapenade, 155
Parmigiano-Reggiano cheese
    Basil and Potato Frittata with Frisée,
       124
    Chicken with Tomato, Basil, and
       Crispy Parmigiano Crackers, 194
    Garlicky Lemon Shrimp, 41
    Linguine alla Carbonara, 147
    Parmigiano Chicken with Molten
       Provolone, 198
    Parmigiano Flounder with White
       Beans and Olive Tapenade, 155
    Prosciutto, Parmigiano, Pimiento, and
       Arugula Salad, 90
    Sausage Lasagna, 148
    Stracciatella, 65
    Warm Artichoke Parmigiano Dip, 29
parsley
    Cannellini with Tricolor Peppers,
       Tomato, and Parsley, 116
    Red, White, and Green Cod, 160
    Shrimp Scampi with Grilled Bread,
       186
pasta
    Capellini alla Puttanesca, 139
    Capellini with Littleneck Clams, 136
    Gnocchi with Toasted Garlic, Walnuts,
       and Bitter Greens, 135
    Handkerchief Pasta with Lobster, Bok
       Choy, and Lemon Cream Sauce, 141
    Linguine alla Carbonara, 147
    Sausage Lasagna, 148
    see also rice noodles
peaches, Pretty Peach Melba, 261
peanut butter, Warm Brownies with a
    Salty Peanut Sauce, 276
peanuts
    Goat Cheese, Radish, and Dried
       Cranberry Salad, 78
    Peanut Chicken and Radicchio Salad,
       86
    Rice Noodles with Spicy Peanut
       Sauce, 134
    Warm Brownies with a Salty Peanut
       Sauce, 276
peanut sauce, Thai. see Thai peanut
    sauce

pears
    Charred Mackerel with Pears and
       Caesar Dressing, 81
    Pear and Stilton Salad, 79
    Pears in Phyllo Cups with Butter
       Pecan Ice Cream and Caramel
       Sauce, 260
peas
    Andouille Sausage Jambalaya with
       Clams and Peas, 231
    Beefy Shepherd's Pie, 223
    Clam Brodettatto with Chorizo and
       Peas, 176
    Sirloin Tips with Gorgonzola Mashed
       Potatoes, 210
    Turkey Chopped Steak with Peas and
       Pickled Onions, 201
peas, snow
    Sautéed Pork with Snow Peas,
       Walnuts, and Beets, 240
    Tangy Turkey and Snow Pea Stir-Fry,
       202
peas, sugar snap, Seared Salmon with
    Sugar Snap Peas and Herring, 169
pecans
    Hot Chicken and Brie Sandwich with
       Toasted Pecans, 94
    Pear and Stilton Salad, 79
pecorino cheese, Grilled Asparagus and
    Oyster Mushrooms with Pecorino
    Cheese, 30
Pecorino-Romano cheese
    Gnocchi with Toasted Garlic, Walnuts,
       and Bitter Greens, 135
    Soft Polenta with Wild Mushrooms, 121
pepper Jack cheese, Broiled Flat-Iron
    Steaks with Pepper Jack Scalloped
    Potatoes, 211
peppers, bell
    Beef Curry Sauté, 217
    Cannellini with Tricolor Peppers,
       Tomato, and Parsley, 116
    Quick Steak, Pizza Man Style, 216
    Tofu and Red Pepper Flash-Fry, 128
peppers, chile
    Fresh Fast Guacamole, 26
    Mushroom and Red Onion Burgers,
       100
    Mushroom Quesadillas, 33
    see also red pepper flakes
peppers, cubanelle, Mamma's Vegetable
    Giambotta, 119
peppers, hot cherry, Warm Chicken, Feta,
    and Melon Seed Pasta Salad, 142
peppers, roasted red, Feta and Kalamata
    Panini, 106
peppers and onions
    Rice Noodles with Spicy Peanut
       Sauce, 134
    Tangy Turkey and Snow Pea Stir-Fry,
       202

phyllo dough
    Chicken and Wild Mushroom Strudel,
       192
    Chocolate Phyllo with Blood Oranges
       and Dulce de Leche Ice Cream, 254
    Pears in Phyllo Cups with Butter
       Pecan Ice Cream and Caramel
       Sauce, 260
    Pretty Peach Melba, 261
    Warm Rice Pudding with Rum Raisin
       Ice Cream, 263
Pico de Gallo Salad with Avocado, 77
Pierogi with Ham, Dandelion Greens,
    and Sour Cream Mustard Sauce, 145
Pigs in a Blanket Swiss Fondue, 59
pimientos
    Prosciutto, Parmigiano, Pimiento, and
       Arugula Salad, 90
    Red, White, and Green Cod, 160
pineapple
    Grilled Pineapple with Cocoa Foam,
       257
    Pineapple French Toast, 273
polenta, Soft Polenta with Wild
    Mushrooms, 121
pomegranate juice, Blueberry
    Pomegranate Consommé with
    Whipped Crème Fraîche, 250
ponzu sauce, New-Style Tuna Sashimi, 34
pork
    Boneless Pork Chops with Potato
       Pancakes and Mustard Greens, 237
    Chilled Pork Tenderloin Salad with
       Chopped Olive Dressing, 89
    Pork and Zucchini Flash-Fry with
       Black Bean Sauce, 239
    Pork Scaloppini Stuffed with Cheddar,
       238
    Sautéed Pork with Snow Peas,
       Walnuts, and Beets, 240
    Stuffed Pork Chops with Boursin and
       Collards, 242
    see also bacon; ham; entries begin-
       ning with "sausage"
potatoes, precooked
    Basil and Potato Frittata with Frisée,
       124
    Beef Shabu-Shabu with Watercress, 71
    Beefy Shepherd's Pie, 223
    Broiled Flat-Iron Steaks with Pepper
       Jack Scalloped Potatoes, 211
    Corned Beef Brisket with Cabbage,
       Potatoes, and Horseradish, 226
    Mamma's Vegetable Giambotta, 119
    Savory Seafood Stew, 174
    Scalloped Potatoes with Gruyère
       Cheese and Mushrooms, 120
    Sirloin Tips with Gorgonzola Mashed
       Potatoes, 210
    Veal Scaloppini in Artichoke Broth,
       227

potato pancakes, Boneless Pork Chops
    with Potato Pancakes and Mustard
    Greens, 237
Pretty Peach Melba, 261
pretzels
    Pretzelized Chicken with Cheddar
        Horseradish Sauce, 199
    Sharp Cheddar and Beer Fondue with
        Warm Pretzels, 50
prosciutto
    Grilled Stuffed Veal with Basil and
        Provolone, 47
    Prosciutto, Mozzarella, and Tomato
        Panini, 109
    Prosciutto, Parmigiano, Pimiento, and
        Arugula Salad, 90
provolone cheese
    Eggplant Parmigiano, 125
    Grilled Stuffed Veal with Basil and
        Provolone, 47
    Parmigiano Chicken with Molten
        Provolone, 198
    12 Eggs in a Pan, 230
prunes, Croissants with Prunes and
        Armagnac, 274
Puffy Chicken with Green Curry Basil
        Sauce, 46
pumpkin puree, Crispy Golden
        Croissants with Pumpkin Cream and
        Candied Ginger, 269

Quesadillas, Mushroom, 33
Quick Steak, Pizza Man Style, 216

radicchio
    Ground Beef with Salsa Verde,
        Radicchio, and Sour Cream, 225
    Peanut Chicken and Radicchio Salad,
        86
radishes
    Goat Cheese, Radish, and Dried
        Cranberry Salad, 78
    New-Style Tuna Sashimi, 34
    Roast Beef and Boursin Panini, 108
raisins, Warm Waldorf Chicken Salad, 88
raspberries
    Chocolate Cakes with Raspberries
        and Nutella Mousse, 267
    Instant Tiramisu with Raspberries,
        258
raspberry sauce, Pretty Peach Melba,
        261
Red, White, and Green Cod, 160
Red Onion Frittata with Baby Spinach,
        126
red pepper flakes
    Capellini with Littleneck Clams, 136
    Shrimp Swiss Fondue with Arrabbiata
        Dipping Sauce, 54
    see also 5-spice powder; peppers,
        chile

relish, chow-chow, Beef Swiss Fondue
    with Three Sauces, 58
relish, garlic
    Roast Beef Wrap with Garlic Relish,
        101
    Turkey Cutlets with Red Kidney
        Beans, Garlic Relish, and
        Watercress, 203
relish, hot dog, Sautéed Pork with Snow
    Peas, Walnuts, and Beets, 240
relish, India, Chicken and Chopped
    Salad, 87
relish, piccalilli, Smoked Salmon and
    Swiss Cheese Panini, 107
rice
    Andouille Sausage Jambalaya with
        Clams and Peas, 231
    Beef and Broccoli-Coleslaw Stir-Fry,
        214
    Beef Curry Sauté, 217
    Catfish and Rice Sofrito, 175
    Chorizo, Smoked Mussel, and Okra
        Rice Pilaf, 235
    Good Ol' Rice and Beans, 118
    Grilled Boneless Leg of Lamb with
        Greek Yogurt Sauce, 244
    Tangy Turkey and Snow Pea Stir-Fry,
        202
rice noodles
    Hot-and-Sour Shrimp Rice Noodle
        Soup, 69
    Puffy Chicken with Green Curry Basil
        Sauce, 46
    Rice Noodles with Spicy Peanut
        Sauce, 134
    Shrimp and Noodle Saté Sauté, 183
    Vietnamese Beef and Basil Soup, 73
    see also pasta
rice pudding, Warm Rice Pudding with
    Rum Raisin Ice Cream, 263
Rich Mushroom Bouillon, 63
ricotta cheese, Classic Cannoli, 268
ricotta salata cheese, Chilled Pork
    Tenderloin Salad with Chopped
    Olive Dressing, 89
Roast Beef, Chestnuts, and Brussels
    Sprouts in Consommé, 222
Roast Beef and Boursin Panini, 108
Roast Beef and Eggplant Alfredo, 220
Roast Beef Borscht, 72
Roast Beef Wrap with Garlic Relish, 101
rosemary, Fried Calamari and Artichokes
    with Hummus Dipping Sauce, 36
rum, Baba au Rum, 265

saffron, Clam Brodettatto with Chorizo
    and Peas, 176
salad dressings, prepared
    Charred Mackerel with Pears and
        Caesar Dressing, 81
    Toasted Hot Dog Reubin, 103

salads
    Avocado Salad with Red Onion and
        Feta, 76
    Buffalo Chicken Tenders with Celery
        and Blue Cheese Salad, 85
    Charred Mackerel with Pears and
        Caesar Dressing, 81
    Chicken, Goat Cheese, and Blood
        Orange Salad, 84
    Chicken and Chopped Salad, 87
    Chilled Pork Tenderloin Salad with
        Chopped Olive Dressing, 89
    Crab Cakes with Avocado Dip and
        Arugula Salad, 178
    Creamy Lemon Shrimp Salad with
        Cucumbers and Watercress, 35
    Goat Cheese, Radish, and Dried
        Cranberry Salad, 78
    Peanut Chicken and Radicchio Salad,
        86
    Pear and Stilton Salad, 79
    Pico de Gallo Salad with Avocado,
        77
    Prosciutto, Parmigiano, Pimiento, and
        Arugula Salad, 90
    Shrimp Salad with Red Onion, Mango,
        and Cilantro, 82
    Tomato and Mozzarella Salad, 80
    Warm Chicken, Feta, and Melon Seed
        Pasta Salad, 142
    Warm Waldorf Chicken Salad, 88
salmon
    Black-and-Tan Salmon with Scallions,
        165
    Honey-Glazed Salmon with Cinnamon,
        Carrots, and Chicory, 166
    Salmon and Sesame Swiss Fondue,
        52
    Salmon in Butternut Squash Barbecue
        Sauce, 167
    Salmon with Shiitake Mushrooms in
        Ginger-Soy Broth, 168
    Seared Salmon with Sugar Snap Peas
        and Herring, 169
salmon, smoked
    Chilled Cucumber Soup with Smoked
        Salmon and Crème Fraîche, 62
    Smoked Salmon and Swiss Cheese
        Panini, 107
salsa
    Curried Mussel Fricassee, 177
    Ground Beef with Refried Beans,
        Salsa, and Grilled Zucchini, 224
    Ground Beef with Salsa Verde,
        Radicchio, and Sour Cream, 225
    Pico de Gallo Salad with Avocado, 77
salsa con queso
    Beef Swiss Fondue with Three Sauces,
        58
    Cheesy Roast Beef and Zucchini, 221
Sashimi, New-Style Tuna, 34

sauerkraut
    Kielbasa and Sauerkraut Stew, 236
    Toasted Hot Dog Reubin, 103
sausage, andouille, Andouille Sausage
    Jambalaya with Clams and Peas, 231
sausage, chorizo
    Chorizo, Smoked Mussel, and Okra
        Rice Pilaf, 235
    Chorizo and Manchego Frittata with
        Mesclun Salad, 233
    Clam Brodettatto with Chorizo and
        Peas, 176
sausage, Italian
    Hot Italian Sausage with Fresh Beans
        and Beets, 234
    Sausage Lasagna, 148
    12 Eggs in a Pan, 230
sausage, kielbasa
    Barbecue Kielbasa with Corn, Black
        Beans, and Corn Muffins, 232
    Kielbasa and Sauerkraut Stew, 236
Sautéed Pork with Snow Peas, Walnuts,
    and Beets, 240
Sautéed Scallops with Pickled Ginger
    Red Cabbage, 179
Savory Seafood Stew, 174
scallions
    Black-and-Tan Salmon with Scallions,
        165
    New-Style Tuna Sashimi, 34
    Roast Beef Borscht, 72
    Sautéed Scallops with Pickled Ginger
        Red Cabbage, 179
    Seared Salmon with Sugar Snap Peas
        and Herring, 169
    Shrimp and Scallion Frittata, 181
    Skewered Shrimp with Beans and
        Scallions, 187
    Tofu and Red Pepper Flash-Fry, 128
    Turkey, Green Onion, and Rice Noodle
        Soup, 70
Scalloped Potatoes with Gruyère Cheese
    and Mushrooms, 120
scallops
    Sautéed Scallops with Pickled Ginger
        Red Cabbage, 179
    See-Thru Scallops with Lemon Brown
        Butter and Celery Leaves, 42
Sea Bass with Leeks, Chestnuts, and
    Dates, 156
Seared Salmon with Sugar Snap Peas
    and Herring, 169
See-Thru Scallops with Lemon Brown
    Butter and Celery Leaves, 42
sesame seeds
    New-Style Tuna Sashimi, 34
    Salmon and Sesame Swiss Fondue, 52
shallots
    All-Purpose Mushroom Mix, 115
    Chilled Cucumber Soup with Smoked
        Salmon and Crème Fraîche, 62

shallots (cont.)
    Rich Mushroom Bouillon, 63
    Soft Scrambled Eggs with Asparagus
        on Toasted Croissants, 127
    Tomato and Mozzarella Salad, 80
Sharp Cheddar and Beer Fondue with
    Warm Pretzels, 50
Shepherd's Pie, Beefy, 223
sherry, Rich Mushroom Bouillon, 63
shrimp
    Creamy Lemon Shrimp Salad with
        Cucumbers and Watercress, 35
    Firecracker Shrimp, 39
    Garlicky Lemon Shrimp, 41
    Hot-and-Sour Shrimp Rice Noodle
        Soup, 69
    Shrimp and Broccoli Flash-Fry, 180
    Shrimp and Noodle Saté Sauté, 183
    Shrimp and Scallion Frittata, 181
    Shrimp Fra Diavolo with Couscous
        and Broccoli Rabe, 182
    Shrimp Salad with Red Onion, Mango,
        and Cilantro, 82
    Shrimp Scampi with Grilled Bread, 186
    Shrimp Swiss Fondue with Arrabbiata
        Dipping Sauce, 54
    Skewered Shrimp with Beans and
        Scallions, 187
Sirloin Tips with Gorgonzola Mashed
    Potatoes, 210
skate, Cornmeal and Red Onion–Crusted
    Skate with Lime Butter, 164
Skewered Shrimp with Beans and
    Scallions, 187
Smoked Salmon and Swiss Cheese
    Panini, 107
S'Mores Tartlets, 262
sofrito seasoning
    Andouille Sausage Jambalaya with
        Clams and Peas, 231
    Catfish and Rice Sofrito, 175
Soft Polenta with Wild Mushrooms, 121
Soft Scrambled Eggs with Asparagus on
    Toasted Croissants, 127
sole
    Savory Seafood Stew, 174
    Sole with Charred Red Onions and
        Lemon Butter, 152
sorbet
    Blueberry Pomegranate Consommé
        with Whipped Crème Fraîche, 250
    Crispy Wonton Wafers with Lemon
        Curd and Strawberries, 259
    Guava Tapioca with Macadamia Nuts,
        271
soups
    Beef Shabu-Shabu with Watercress, 71
    Chilled Cucumber Soup with Smoked
        Salmon and Crème Fraîche, 62
    Corn and Crab Chowder with
        Tarragon, 66

soups (cont.)
    Hot-and-Sour Shrimp Rice Noodle
        Soup, 69
    Mushroom Soup with Boursin
        Croutons, 64
    Rich Mushroom Bouillon, 63
    Roast Beef Borscht, 72
    Stracciatella, 65
    Thai Bling-Bling Soup, 275
    Turkey, Green Onion, and Rice Noodle
        Soup, 70
    Vietnamese Beef and Basil Soup, 73
sour cream
    Chicken and Wild Mushroom Strudel,
        192
    Chicken Swiss Fondue with Dijon Sour
        Cream and Hummus, 56
    Ground Beef with Salsa Verde,
        Radicchio, and Sour Cream, 225
    Mushroom Quesadillas, 33
    Pierogi with Ham, Dandelion Greens,
        and Sour Cream Mustard Sauce, 145
    Roast Beef Borscht, 72
spinach
    Pretzelized Chicken with Cheddar
        Horseradish Sauce, 199
    Red Onion Frittata with Baby Spinach,
        126
squid
    Fried Calamari and Artichokes with
        Hummus Dipping Sauce, 36
    Grilled Squid with Coconut Broth,
        Leeks, and Papaya, 171
starfruit, Guava Tapioca with Macadamia
    Nuts, 271
steak sauce, Broiled Flat-Iron Steaks
    with Pepper Jack Scalloped
    Potatoes, 211
stews
    Kielbasa and Sauerkraut Stew, 236
    Savory Seafood Stew, 174
Stilton cheese, Pear and Stilton Salad,
    79
stir-fry dishes
    Beef and Broccoli-Coleslaw Stir-Fry,
        214
    Grilled Flank Steak with Shredded
        Carrots and Pickled Ginger, 213
    Tangy Turkey and Snow Pea Stir-Fry,
        202
    see also flash-fry dishes
stir-fry sauce
    Beef and Broccoli-Coleslaw Stir-Fry,
        214
    Grilled Flank Steak with Shredded
        Carrots and Pickled Ginger, 213
Stracciatella, 65
strawberries
    Crispy Wonton Wafers with Lemon
        Curd and Strawberries, 259
    S'Mores Tartlets, 262

Stuffed Pork Chops with Boursin and Collards, 242
stuffing mix, Turkey, Broccoli, and Cheese Casserole, 206
succotash, Barbecue Kielbasa with Corn, Black Beans, and Corn Muffins, 232
sunflower seeds, Chicken, Goat Cheese, and Blood Orange Salad, 84
Swiss cheese
    Smoked Salmon and Swiss Cheese Panini, 107
    Toasted Hot Dog Reubin, 103

taco shells, Ground Beef with Refried Beans, Salsa, and Grilled Zucchini, 224
Taleggio cheese, Golden Chicken and Taleggio Cutlets, 197
tamari soy sauce
    Salmon and Sesame Swiss Fondue, 52
    Salmon with Shiitake Mushrooms in Ginger-Soy Broth, 168
    Tuna Tempura Swiss Fondue with Wasabi Soy, 53
Tangy Turkey and Snow Pea Stir-Fry, 202
tapenade, Parmigiano Flounder with White Beans and Olive Tapenade, 155
tapioca pudding
    Guava Tapioca with Macadamia Nuts, 271
    Thai Bling-Bling Soup, 275
tarragon
    Corn and Crab Chowder with Tarragon, 66
    Mahi-Mahi with Endive and Orange Marmalade Glaze, 170
    Mushroom Fondue, 51
    Soft Scrambled Eggs with Asparagus on Toasted Croissants, 127
teriyaki sauce, Beef and Onion Flash-Fry, 215
Thai Bling-Bling Soup, 275
Thai green curry paste, Puffy Chicken with Green Curry Basil Sauce, 46
Thai hot curry paste
    Beef Curry Sauté, 217
    Curried Mussel Fricassee, 177
    Hot-and-Sour Shrimp Rice Noodle Soup, 69
Thai peanut sauce
    Duck and Eggplant Flash-Fry, 207
    Peanut Chicken and Radicchio Salad, 86
    Rice Noodles with Spicy Peanut Sauce, 134
    Shrimp and Noodle Saté Sauté, 183

thyme
    All-Purpose Mushroom Mix, 115
    Chicken and Wild Mushroom Strudel, 192
    Rich Mushroom Bouillon, 63
    Soft Polenta with Wild Mushrooms, 121
    Veal Scaloppini in Artichoke Broth, 227
Tiramisu, Instant, with Raspberries, 258
Toasted Hot Dog Reubin, 103
Tofu and Red Pepper Flash-Fry, 128
tomatoes
    Chicken with Tomato, Basil, and Crispy Parmigiano Crackers, 194
    Cod Provençal, 159
    Prosciutto, Mozzarella, and Tomato Panini, 109
    Tomato and Mozzarella Salad, 80
tomato paste, Cannellini with Tricolor Peppers, Tomato, and Parsley, 116
tomato puree, Mamma's Vegetable Giambotta, 119
tortilla chips, Fresh Fast Guacamole, 26
tortillas, Mushroom Quesadillas, 33
Trout with Butternut Squash and Blood Oranges, 162–63
tuna
    New-Style Tuna Sashimi, 34
    Tuna Tempura Swiss Fondue with Wasabi Soy, 53
turkey
    Hot Turkey "Coleslaw" Sandwich, 96
    Tangy Turkey and Snow Pea Stir-Fry, 202
    Turkey, Broccoli, and Cheese Casserole, 206
    Turkey, Green Onion, and Rice Noodle Soup, 70
    Turkey Chopped Steak with Peas and Pickled Onions, 201
    Turkey Cutlets with Red Kidney Beans, Garlic Relish, and Watercress, 203
turnip greens, Gnocchi with Toasted Garlic, Walnuts, and Bitter Greens, 135
12 Eggs in a Pan, 230

veal
    Grilled Stuffed Veal with Basil and Provolone, 47
    Veal Scaloppini in Artichoke Broth, 227
Vietnamese Beef and Basil Soup, 73
Vietnamese chili garlic sauce, Firecracker Shrimp, 39

walnuts
    Dutch Apples on Challah with Maple-Walnut Sauce, 270

walnuts (cont.)
    Gnocchi with Toasted Garlic, Walnuts, and Bitter Greens, 135
    Miso-Walnut Chicken with Rainbow Swiss Chard, 200
    Sautéed Pork with Snow Peas, Walnuts, and Beets, 240
Warm Artichoke Parmigiano Dip, 29
Warm Brownies with a Salty Peanut Sauce, 276
Warm Chicken, Feta, and Melon Seed Pasta Salad, 142
Warm Rice Pudding with Rum Raisin Ice Cream, 263
Warm Waldorf Chicken Salad, 88
wasabi paste, Tuna Tempura Swiss Fondue with Wasabi Soy, 53
watercress
    Beef Shabu-Shabu with Watercress, 71
    Creamy Lemon Shrimp Salad with Cucumbers and Watercress, 35
    Fennel-Seared Chicken Livers with Watercress and Oranges, 44
    Turkey Cutlets with Red Kidney Beans, Garlic Relish, and Watercress, 203
whiskey, Fresh Oranges with Jack Daniel's and Yogurt, 272
White Bean and Mushroom Chili, 129
wine
    All-Purpose Mushroom Mix, 115
    Clam Brodettatto with Chorizo and Peas, 176
    Mushroom Fondue, 51
    Mussels with Hummus Broth and Crusty Italian Bread, 38
    Quick Steak, Pizza Man Style, 216
wonton skins, Crispy Wonton Wafers with Lemon Curd and Strawberries, 259

yogurt
    Fresh Oranges with Jack Daniel's and Yogurt, 272
    Grilled Boneless Leg of Lamb with Greek Yogurt Sauce, 244
    Roast Beef Wrap with Garlic Relish, 101

zucchini
    Cheesy Roast Beef and Zucchini, 221
    Grilled Lamb with Sweet-and-Sour Cranberry Sauce, 245
    Ground Beef with Refried Beans, Salsa, and Grilled Zucchini, 224
    Pork and Zucchini Flash-Fry with Black Bean Sauce, 239
    Savory Seafood Stew, 174
    12 Eggs in a Pan, 230
zucchini cakes, Sautéed Scallops with Pickled Ginger Red Cabbage, 179